From the Books of

Greek and Etruscan Painting

History of Art

Title page illustration:

Italiot krater
The Vase of the Persians (detail)
Middle 4th century B.C.
Naples, National Museum

Cover illustration:

Alabaster sarcophagus
From Haghia Triada Crete
Detail of a Religious Ceremony
Cretan art, 14th century B.C.
Archaeological Museum, Heraclion

Greek and Etruscan Painting

Tony Spiteris

Heron Books

Series edited by Claude Schaeffner
Artistic adviser:
Jean-Clarence Lambert
Illustrations chosen by André Held
Assistant: Martine Caputo
Cartographer: Jacques Ricci
Translated by Janet Sondheimer

The colour illustrations in the first part were supplied by Andre Held, Lausanne, including the cover
illustration.

The illustrations in black-and-white in the dictionary were supplied by:
Andre Held: pages 150, 155, 158, 161, 165, 167,
170, 172, 173, 178, 191, 197 and 202;
Roger-Viollet, Paris: pages 146, 152, 153, 156,
158, 160 right, 176, 177, 180, 183, 184, 185, 190,
193 and 194;
Giraudon, Paris: pages 148, 149, 175, 187, 188,
and 203;
Alinari-Giraudon, Paris: pages 160 left and 196;
Anderson-Giraudon, Paris: page 158.

Table of contents

Introduction

Nothing of major classical painting has come down to us. If the history of western art is visualised as a pyramid, at its base there is nothing but an enormous blank.

Nevertheless, the ancient writers were just as enthusiastic over the paintings of their time as they were over the sculptures of Polykleitos and Pheidias. But they are known to us only from scenes painted on the sides of fifth century Attic vases and the frescoes of Etruscan tombs, dim reflections of the pictures which adorned the temples or were displayed in the Parthenon. One proof of the importance, richness and variety of this art, whose birth remains an enigma, is surely the influence it exerted as it spread out over the Mediterranean world, an influence maintained throughout the Later Roman Empire and continued later in Byzantium. Again, in formulating their theories about art, did not Plato and Aristotle rely as much on the works of painters as of poets?

Basing his propositions on his own conception of "mimesis", Plato logically deduced from it that art should be condemned. Aristotle, on the contrary, holding "mimesis" to be a manifestation of intelligence, made it the basis of his poetics and enunciated the new principles of aesthetics. To condemn, Plato declared himself the upholder of a distinction between the faculties of understanding and of feeling, between the idea and the real image, rejecting the ancient notion which made the idea and the image one and the same, expressed, moreover, by the same word: "eidos".

Thus for Democritus there was co-ordination between the two faculties, and the image, or representation, was the very essence of nature. This was not the concept of the essence of art as based upon reason and dissimulated under an illusory appearance, a concept which had not yet been formulated at this period; rather, it was the concept which accepts that the image, as it forms in the mind of a man observing what lies about him, represents not a precise object but the ensemble of everything visible. With this meaning, the idea-image comes close to myth, which represents less the sum of religious beliefs than an ensemble, composed, too, of poetic and figurative images.

Now if the philosophies of Plato and Aristotle are inseparable from their knowledge of art as it evolved in their homeland, it seems that one can with all likelihood affirm:

1. that Plato knew of the period at which painting presented itself as the projection of the visible "eidos", the idea-image;

2. that if he is at pains to criticise the refusal to separate the idea (intelligence) from the image (sensation), it must be because he has before him painting which adopts another mode of expression and distinguishes between the idea, philosophical thought, and the image, sensible reality;

3. that his condemnation of art refers to this painting, which he judges inferior because it is only a copy;

4. that Aristotle, endowing "mimesis" with the value of an intellectual action, locates the essence of art, and of painting in particular, in the knowledge of sensible reality, in a word of nature.

This philosophical debate, turning on the concept of "mimesis", corresponds to

7

Nestor
François Tomb, Vulci
Fresco (detail)
Rome, Museo Torlonia

the actual conflict which, as we well know, was taking place over Greek sculpture from the sixth century down to the time of Lysippos; but there are strong reasons for believing that it corresponded even more closely to the debate in painting over the question of reproducing the image, the real appearance.

It is impossible to suppose that in the Greek mind the distinction between painting and sculpture was founded on colour and relief alone, since the sculptures were coloured. If the Greeks had thought of "mimesis" as the imitation of nature, sculpture would have been considered more perfect than painting, more faithful, more complete. From what we know, they thought nothing of the kind, for it is clear that the absence of relief was considered one of the virtues of painting and not a defect. In effect, if the artist does not reproduce but "produces" an image, this itself becomes a reality, not a copy of reality, and will be all the closer and more faithful to reality if it refrains from stressing the physical side of reality, which does not exist.

Although drawn from reality, in coming to birth a pictorial work creates its own dimensions, which prevent it from becoming embroiled in those of ordinary space. Sculpture, too, avoids this point of physical contact since it comes to occupy architectonic space—pediments, colonnades, the "cella" of the temple—and protects itself by its polychrome covering or, when made of bronze, by repelling the light from its dark surface, which is hard and full of reflections. Painting is more intransigent still, and it is not true to say—in the archaic period at least—that it extends over a plane, a spatial entity. In projecting itself over a plane, the painting destroys it: in painting, the plane is an imaginary plane, like that on which the ideas, or more precisely the "phantasms", of the mind are projected.

Polygnotos, who lived before Plato, was celebrated by the writers as an "ethno-graphos", that is to say an artist capable of understanding the "ethos" of his models and revealing their virtues or defects, but it was also said of him that knew how to leave the particular forms of bodies to be guessed at beneath the draperies which covered them. These observations are not contradictory, for they characterise an artist who seems to have gone beyond slavish representation. Study of paintings from several of the potters' workshops is edifying in this connection since the scenes on certain vases have obviously been modelled on subjects treated by Polygnotos in his pictures. The people, isolated from one another, are disposed on different planes and describe individual gestures unrelated, to what others are doing. In this space, with no indication of perspective or relief, there is normally a complete absence of artificial shading or coloured transparency to suggest the corporal forms beneath the opaqueness of the drapery. Polygnotos drew in this way: body and draperies were one, just as the man and his "ethos" were united. Had he intended to paint concrete, realistic figures, with their bodily structure, by placing them in an exact location he would have had to draw in all their surroundings, what was above and below them; but his aim was to make visible an idea, an abstraction which had no need of anything exterior whatsoever.

The Elder Pliny, drawing on Greek sources, praises Parrhasios for having

8

adopted "the rule of symmetry" in painting and for knowing how to trace the contours of bodies "making evident the hidden forms". Polygnotos did not share this aim, and for him it was not a question of rigorously representing draperies and bodies but of making one feel, thanks to the line of his drawing, that the model is something other than one sees. If Polygnotos can be compared with the sculptors of the pediments for the temple of Aegina or Olympia, of Parrhasios it is relevant to remark that he was the friend and collaborator of Pheidias. For knowledge of him we are again indebted to some pottery vases: certain white-ground "lekythoi" are marked with the severe beauty of his drawing, whose line, independent of colour, succeeds unaided in defining the mystery hidden behind the image, in giving a clear account of a purely abstract idea.

Aristotle will confront the consummate beauty of the figures of Zeuxis and the severity of those of Parrhasios. At the beginning of the fourth century Parrhasios was already classed with the ancients, while Zeuxis was considered a modern. For the philosophers, to speak of beauty already entails comparing nature—from which the ideal forms should be chosen— with the works of the painters. In praising Zeuxis, Lucian extols the novelty of his methods, Quintilian his skill in rendering the effects of light, and Pliny considers him the artistic successor of Apollodoros Skiagraphos, the painter of shadows. This time the potters' workshops provide no copies, since Zeuxis' chiaroscuro effects did not lend themselves to reproduction on vase surfaces by the craft techniques of the ceramic artists.

Zeuxis can most surely be compared with Praxiteles, the sculptor who more than any other set himself to render immanent truth. For him, "the beautiful" was not an "archetypal idea" but a choice between natural appearances, and he has left proof of the extreme refinement of his taste.

Zeuxis is the inverse of Parrhasios, placing sensation before intellectual values and appearance above the idea; more precisely, he seeks to explain and present the person as a person, neither elevating him to an abstraction nor degrading him to make him a base material object. This problem of the material object, or of the figure considered as an object, will be posed only later, at Rome. For Zeuxis—and this is why his work is cited as an example of perfect "mimesis"—the question did not exist. His aim, the same as the one which Lysippos the sculptor set himself a little later, was to paint things not as they are but as they appeared to him, that is to say, as pure imaginings.

We shall find that Apelles, the most illustrious painter at the court of Alexander the Great, is drawn not towards the severe Platonic tendencies of Parrhasios but to the theories of Zeuxis. By this time, major painting and the miniatures of the potteries no longer had anything in common: ceramic, which had reached the level of "minor art", descended again to that of the purely "decorative". Apelles declared that having first followed the canons of the "beautiful" according to Zeuxis and Praxiteles, he had abandoned them, to seek out freer forms which permitted him to enliven the stories he was fond of illustrating with variegated colours, skilfully modulated. Having been merely a kind of "photography", painting identified itself with the mental activity which brings an image to birth, in a word with the imagination. The images produced by sensory shock are no different from those which are born by mnemotechnical methods. Nature is what she is, but she can be a moment of the imagination which develops freely in space and time.

Painting which takes its inspiration from nature will enrich its sense of allegory. Hellenic allegorism acts not by transposition proceeding from the concept to the image, but rather by what could be called "transparency". The more life-like the representation, the more readily it allows unlooked for fictions to show through. Nature properly speaking, and her subterranean universe, are in sum nothing but the supreme and total image of the world, under which all the allegories can be built. The starting point of the great stream of Greek art is its naturalism, so often celebrated, which can be summed up as adopting the world as the boundless property of the imagination. After the coming of Christ, Byzantine art, in which painting is nothing else than the reflection of divinity, will emerge from this same matrix.

It is to Greek painting, rather than to the miniatures of Attic vases or the walls of funerary chambers sprawling with the sultry Etruscan frescoes, that one must look to discover the nature of this great vanished civilisation. Its influence on the Western world was immense, and the value of historical events is to be judged more by their effects on the past than by their immediate repercussions.

Giulio Carlo Argan

Greek painting

The natural setting of the birth and unfolding of one of the most original civilisations the world has ever known has remained virtually unchanged since antiquity.

An eye which could take in at a glance this part of Mediterranean Europe together with the peninsula surrounded by its constellations of islands, would see a verdant zone which descends from the massif of the Rhodope* range, shades with its tints of gold the fertile plains of Macedonia, clambers up Olympus* and Pindus,* spills over into the fields of Thessaly, caressing their fairness, to lose itself finally in the Ionian sea. A second zone, composed of ochres, winds itself round the shores of Attica, spreads out in grey and mauve to cross the isthmus, climbs the blood-red hills of the gulf of Corinth* and finally disappears behind the Peloponnese,* with touches of olive-green on the Taygetus.* Surrounding all is the marvellous crown of an uninterrupted chain of islets. These are the islands of the Aegean,* whose abstract whiteness interweaves with the emerald blues of the Cretan archipelago, until the Ionian is reached, with its seven isles plunged in green. And all these ochres, greys and whites are bathed in the deep blue of the sea, in an ethereal, diaphanous, immaterial light which blots out details, allowing the masses and grand planes to emerge. This is the range of colours, the palette which will confront us in all the pictorial records of the past.

But in Greece nature is rich in many other elements. The graphic quality of the line determining the rhythm constitutes a base factor. Unique and pure, uniform in its trueness, multiple in its details, undulant, space embraces it, moulds it, simplifies it, transforms it into an element of music. There is rhythmical repetition, which binds the blue of the sky visible between the columns of the Parthenon to the whiteness of the fluting, the sluggish, measured chant of the sea to the continuity of the mountains.

And then the entire Greek landscape is imprinted with an element whose very essence is power and terror: the drama—the heritage from the gods. Every corner of this land is immured in tragedy. Bare and rugged mountains, burnt by the implacable sun; small volcanic islands, their rocks eroded by the salt sea and the on-shore winds. Vigorous thrusting light penetrates the secret of the most sequestered places. Impressive Mycenaean emptiness, where silence follows after the tragedy of the Atrides, where the solitary croaking of ravens is heard, eerie reminder of the Pythian prophecies.

Other countries are tragic. But their harsh and unyielding character destroys humanity. The tragedy of this land has been nourished on human suffering. It keeps this character, through its symphathy with man and the human scale. The drama is confined within the space in which men live and suffer, never assuming a metaphysical significance. For at the root and origin of good and evil, of beauty and ugliness, lie the feelings, desires and passions of men.

An asterisk after a word refers to the dictionary where the word is the subject of an article or reference. Unless otherwise stated all dates in this book are B.C.

Cretan civilisation

The first traces of habitation on Crete,* whose civilisation is the most ancient in the Aegean, date only from the neolithic age. As Aristotle remarks, Crete "dominates the sea round which all the Hellenes have settled", and it is along the coasts that the earliest imhabitants make their homes, engaging in husbandry, hunting and fishing. They make implements, hatchets from sandstone, weapons and tools from bone and stone. They use obsidian imported from Melos for their knives and arrow points. Their somewhat crude pottery is polished by hand. The Cretans worship the fertility goddess, represented in clay or soapstone statuettes with protuberant breasts and enormous flanks.

Thirty centuries pass in this way, until in about the year 3000 the Pelasgi invade the Aegean. Now metal makes its appearance, weapons and cutting instruments will be made of copper, ornaments of gold or silver. Crete becomes the scene of a new civilisation, based on familiar groups, which will last for five or six centuries. Taste becomes more refined and huts slowly give way to huge decorated houses. Evidence of this mode of life comes from seals engraved with ideograms. As time passes more obvious advances are made. The Cretan thalassocracy* is becoming a reality. Mariners bring back precious objects from their long coastal voyages, ivory, syenite vases from Egypt, idols of marble from the Cyclades, obsidian from Melos, metals and marbles from neighbouring islands. Industry improves. The primitive vases—vivid colours on a dark background—will now be flamed. Progress is made with sculpting in stone and ivory.

For Crete, the Bronze Age is undoubtedly the great age of its civilisation. Halfway to Cyprus, where copper was being exploited, facing the Cyclades, which was a source of tin, equidistant from Egypt and Troy,* Crete soon becomes the centre of a bronze industry which will bring wealth, technical experience and a flourishing trade, underwritten by a maritime supremacy which will endure for six centuries.

Large towns are founded, points of interchange between the two coasts of the island: Knossos,* facing the Cyclades and the Argolis, and Phaestos,* from which the dark-prowed ships leave for Egypt.

Around the year 2000 the kings erect palaces to match their opulence, in which princely apartments, sanctuaries dedicated to divinities, shops and craftshops follow one upon another. These palaces are adorned with colonnades and frescoes. Around them, the straggling villages multiply, houses with several storeys spring up. Unlike the peasants, the urban population enjoys a life of luxury, indulging in sports and games of chance, taking part in the many festivities and light-hearted entertainments, assisting devoutly at the religious ceremonies. There is intense activity in the royal workshops and increasing perfection in their products. The daggers, in varying shapes, become covered with chasings. The engravers cut human and animal figures on gems.

With lathes at their disposal, the potters make vases with walls thin as metal, which they cover with bright, variegated colours. Kamares,* one of the most beautiful of all pottery styles, now makes its appearance. Trade is still on the increase. Luxury ceramic wares travel as far as upper Egypt, silver vases are sought after in Byblos, soapstone vases in the Argolis and Phocis;* spices are imported from Cyrenaica.

But this happy existence is doomed to be blighted by disaster. At some time around 1750,[1] the villages crumble, the splendid palaces are buried under ash. Knossos, Phaestos, Mallia,* Tylissos* are now nothing but ruins. What happened? The experts are still unable to provide a satisfatcory explanation.

But this happy existence is doomed to be blighted by disaster. At some time around 1750,[1] the villages crumble, the splendid palaces are buried under ash. Knossos, Phaestos, Mallia,* Tylissos* are now nothing but ruins. What happened? The experts are still unable to provide a satisfactory explanation. One theory speaks of Asiatic invasions, another of an earthquake followed by a revolution. This last hypothesis appears to have more in its favour.

Cretan ewer from Phaistos (detail)
Leaf motif
16th-15th century B.C.
Museum at Heraklion

Mycenaean civilisation

It was long thought that Mycenaean civilisation arose merely in consequence of colonisation by the Cretans after the disaster to the island in the seventeenth century. It is true that during this period a radical transformation can be observed in the Argolis, now emerging from its rural stage and reflecting Cretan influence in its customs, religious practices and arts. The women adopt the fashions of Knossos. In the sanctuaries, the mother-goddess is worshipped with her familiar attributes and the dead wear masks of gold and precious jewels. Sumptuous princely dwellings, adorned with frescoes, are being built on the mainland.

Many indeed are the scholars who have endeavoured to account for the appearance of this metamorphosis, some inclining to the theory of a slow and peaceful penetration, others explaining it as the result of a princely subsidy paid to the Achaeans by the Egyptians, in return for assistance which led to the expulsion of the Hyksos

Mycenaean krater
War-gear of warriors
13th century B.C.
Athens, National Museum

dynasty. Both theses seem equally valid. This civilisation, as assimilated and transformed by the Archaeans, will dominate Hellas for two centuries. The vases in the "palace style" and the building of chamber or domed tombs confirms that the penetration was progressive.

The catastrophe which smites the Cretan cities confirms the Mycenaean hegemony and removes the centre of the Aegean world to the Argolis. The Achaeans are now powerful and without rivals; henceforth their will, their way of life and their artists will be imposed on the rest of Greece. From Orchomenos* to Athens,* from Thebes* as far as Macedonia the same objects crop up, the same shapes of vases, the same techniques of working metal, ivories, weapons and gems. All bear the imprint of a single civilisation. Hellas has taken shape and matches the descriptions given by the poet of the Iliad.

But in spreading over the land and along the Mediterranean coasts the Achaeans become dispersed, their fortified places dismantled. In 1229 their expedition to the Nile delta is a disaster. Invaders from Illyria, taking advantage of Achaean weakness, accomplish their ruin, and amid fire and blood plunge Hellas into four centuries of darkness and silence.

Creto-Mycenaean art

It is only among a people of refined aesthetic sense that artists express themselves with such freedom and power of expression, with an acute observation of nature, whose details are captured in spare, simplified, ideographic strokes. Cretans felt the attraction of colour as early as the third millennium, covering the walls of their houses with red painting, applied over a layer of fine plaster. Later on, with technical improvement and the introduction of pure lime as a coating, the artist "resumes" the natural image in a rapid sketch with no retouching, preserving its essence and discarding detail, in contrast with the precious minuteness shown by the Egyptians.

The first palaces of Knossos and Phaestos were decorated with polychrome drawings with lively tonal qualities. Giving free rein to their imagination, the artists soon enriched their repertory with plant or animal forms; but a dominant place was reserved for the human being. Among the most ancient documents is a fragment of fresco discovered at Phylakopi* (Melos), in which fish can be seen skimming the waves in all directions. The "Crocus gatherer" belongs to this same epoch.

In the following period, profiting from long experience, the painter can make better use of his means of expression. He sticks to the conventional colours, borrowed from the Egyptians: bronzed flesh for the men, white for the women. He knows nothing of chiaroscuro, his colours are applied as flat washes. Projections are isometric, eyes are still drawn frontally even if the face is in profile, limbs are omitted or given sum-

Minet el-Beida
Mycenaean vase, fragment
13th century B.C.
Paris, Louvre

Mycenaean krater (detail)
Line of warriors
13th century B.C.
Athens, National Museum

mary treatment. The graceful head known as "La Parisienne" lacks ears. Yet despite these weaknesses, the direct rendering, spontaneity in movement and chromatic harmony give their works a naive charm. Skilful draftsmen, acute observers, the Cretans delight in stressing the beauty of noble ladies, the grace of their prince, the elegance of their clothing. The landscape artists illustrate with a light brush and exquisite taste the simple life of the reed-bed, a carpet of white lilies. Others draw their inspiration from animals, captured in their most characteristic pose: for example, the watchful cat ready to pounce on a pheasant, represented on a fragment discovered at Hagia Triada.

Then a new type of painting emerges, the miniature fresco. The artist applies himself with verve and relish to the description of genre scenes, events from daily life reducing them to scale he shows the skill of the seal engraver or the goblet chaser. Fascinated by movement, he becomes excited over a scene from the bull contest: the beast charges with lowered head, the toreador in a single movement seizes him by the horns and steps aside while an acrobat executes a somersault on the animal's back.

Some fifty years later the small format is abandoned and there is a return to large-scale compositions. But these lack force, the drawing becomes finical, the motifs recur and become stylised. The two gryphons from the throne-room at Knossos or the large "Procession" fresco, in which long-robed women and loin-clothed young men advance in hieratic fashion demonstrate that the artist knew no better than to repeat a single prototype, in a monotonous, almost academic manner.

The Hagia Triada sarcophagus is a happy exception. The most complete ensemble to come down to us, it depicts sundry episodes in a religious ceremony: youths bringing their offering to the god, a sacrifice, yoke-bearing women. Incomparable in style and highly coloured, the work astonishes by its thought-out composition, the liveliness of the facial expressions, the refreshing variety of solutions to a subject so often treated. True, the artist respects traditional techniques, but he has tried to convey some idea of space by diminishing the objects furthest away. A millennium will pass before we encounter another innovation of this nature, among the Greeks of the archaic period.

Crete apart, there is no trace of mural painting in any region before the seventeenth century. The murals of Amnisos date from about 1600, the palace frieze at Thebes from 1450, while the frescoes of Mycenae, Tiryns, Orchomenos and Pylos are much later still. The technique, the evolved conception in the style of these frescoes betray the influence of Cretan emigrants. The subjects are inspired by the habits of the great island, and the scenes of hunting or warfare which gratified the bellicose temper of the great lords are numerous.

In this new continental setting the art of fresco continues to prosper. With the disappearance of the Cretan workshops, it asserts a character of its own and blooms in complete independence. Painters adapt their style more and more to the requirements and tastes of their new masters, devotees of vast, animated compositions.

◄Cretan rhyton
(Drinking vase)
16th-15th century B.C.
Museum at Heraklion

Cretan pitcher   ►
Kamares style
19th-18th century B.C.
Museum at Heraklion

Painted relief

The painted relief is characteristic of Cretan art and found nowhere else in the Mediterranean. The earliest examples date from the seventeenth century, but the finest come from the sixteenth and fifteenth. The procedure was to block out the pattern on a clay plaster and then finish it in hard stucco. Some rank among the most significant masterpieces of Minoan art, for example the majestic and impressive king-priest bearing the insignia of his office—crown and fleur-de-lys collar—whose image adorned a wall in the long corridor of Processions in the palace at Knossos.

These relief frescoes, wonderfully appropriate to large surfaces, had as their themes scenes from the bull-contest, games, processions, and were crowded with people.

Pottery

The essential characteristics we have seen determining the activity of the creators of mural painting can be met with again among the craftsmen potters. Although these two techniques are quite closely related, the connection between them will still be less intimate than among the Greeks.

The fact is that the Cretans subordinate their ornamentation to the validation

22

Cretan amphora (detail)
Octopus
15th century B.C.
Athens, National Museum

of form. These vases lack the qualities of rhythm, measure and proportion which lend
such perfection to Hellenic pottery. The formal weakness will thus be compensated by
the decorative contribution, with its accent on plasticity. This explains the tendency
towards geometrism or simplification of the elements, even those derived from nature,
leading to an inevitable stylisation.

Contrary to what happened in the Cyclades, the natural aesthetic sense of the
Cretans leads them by instinct to ennoble a purely utilitarian manufacture, making
of it a luxury art. They will also profit from technical advances such as the invention
of the lathe or kiln improvements, as also from the discovery of bronze, to bring
diversity into their shapes and decoration. The taste of the consumer, whether their
own kings or the distant clientele on the mainland or the islands, will also be a guide.

From 2800, following the example of metallurgy, the potter works with kilns
at very high temperatures, which enables him to achieve new colourings, vitrification
effects and a great variety of shapes, thanks to the ever-increasing malleability of his
materials. Later on the drawing becomes more supple and the straight line is replaced
by a curve. Once the spiral has been adopted from the Cyclades, curvilinear and
spiroidal motifs make their appearance, as also the "flamed" vases in the style known
as Vasiliki, in which the red or orange coating is mottled with black and bronzed
flecks. It also becomes possible to throw footed cups, ewers, and long-spouted pitchers,
known as "theieroi". At the end of this period the craftsman becomes more audacious
still and invents jars of enormous size, pithoi.

The princely builders of the first palaces give pottery a new impetus. They take
23

Cretan fresco, provenance Knossos
Prince with Fleur de Lis
16th century B.C.
Museum at Heraklion

Knossos
Fragment of a Cretan fresco
Head of a young girl, known as *La Parisienne*
About 16th century B.C.
Museum at Heraklion

the humble potters under their protection, installing them under their own roofs and supplying them with the improved material of the day. The slowly revolving lathe, a new invention, allows the craftsman to work in safety on the very thin-walled vases, often less than a millimetre thick, known as "egg-shell". Increasingly, the potter looks to objects made in bronze or precious metal for inspiration in turning his elegant cups or goblets. An earthen-ware cantharus has been found at Gournia side by side with its silver model. New colours appear: a more viscous black, which turns purple after firing; a liquid white which goes ivory; and the gamut of reds is enriched. The finest ware, the efflorescence of the polychrome style, is in the style known as Kamares, from the cave in which the first examples were discovered. The linear and curvilinear drawings are various in the extreme. The stylised vegetable motifs marry with the shape of the vase, and accentuate it still further by their chromatic richness.

The ceramic artist is led by his own taste for colour, coupled with Egyptian example, to make new experiments, which will results in the discovery of faience ware. Soon he will be able to produce blue vases with gilded mounting.

But the catastrophe which brings about the ruin of the earliest palaces also deprives the craftsmen of their royal clientele, obliging them to work for classes of less cultivated taste. Colours lose their brightness, plant motifs are reduced to geometrical simplification and the ware which still shows the potters at their best is the "ribbed" pottery, imitating tortoise-shell.

During the sixteenth century new palaces are in building, finer and more sumptuous than their predecessors. Their adornment and decoration are entrusted to the great artists of the day, who use a flowery style to depict scenes from princely life.

A whole new world of plants, animals and human beings opens up to the astonished gaze of the craftsmen, who transpose it in attenuated form to their vases. Naturalism has triumphed. At first, the painting is done in white on a brown lilac ground, the drawing is lively, with some almost impressionistic features. On the large jars, slender and harmonious in shape, there is a return to the favourite motifs, flowers—lilies above all—or marine animals, in which the tentacles of octopoi readily take the place of spirals.

Eventually, this naturalism is schematised. Linear motifs intermingle with the flowers and fishes. In order to intensify the decorative effect, and in imitation of major painting, the vase is divided up into horizontal zones, decorated with different motifs. Towards the middle of the fifteenth century there is thus a convergence with the "palace style". One of the finest examples is a jar from the royal villa at Knossos, painted on relief and richly decorated.

In the other parts of the Aegean world, and at Mycenae, the evolution of pottery follows an almost identical curve. However, during the last phase of the Mycenaean era the accent is on schematisation, and decoration dwindles to vague and abstract strokes. The only surviving traces of the sumptuous art of the preceding centuries are all but unrecognisable.

Cretan vase
Bird and fish
14th century B.C.
Museum at Heraklion

The origins of Greek art

Towards the end of the second millennium before our era, Greece is invaded by war-like peoples from Central Europe, who spread fire and blood in their wake. For Mycenaean civilisation, this is the final blow. For centuries, insecurity and poverty will be the order of the day, producing a climate unfavourable to the blossoming of art in any form. During this dark age, a shadow seems to fall over the Greek world. Even if tradition appears to be maintained as regards religion, habitation, language and crafts, writing as such disappears almost completely.

It was long thought that there was a complete break between Mycenaean art and that of the geometric period. Today we are in a position to affirm the existence of a certain affinity between them. The newcomers belonged to the same race, spoke the same language and in their works were strongly influenced by reality, which predisposed them to a schematic view of things and pointed the way towards order and rationalism.

At the beginning of the tenth century one observes a change in aesthetic concepts. The revival starts in Attica, and its spread to the rest of Greece appears to keep pace with the progress of the invaders as they settle and become assimilated with the local populations.

Pottery provides the best guide to the evolution of style at this epoch: partly because we possess such a large number of documents, which makes it possible to establish an approximate chronology, and partly because of its more pronounced feeling for geometric decoration, so characteristic of the period.

The geometric style reproduces nature by simplifying it. The craftsman is feeling his way, as it were, and allows himself to be guided by instinct. He makes much use of the straight line, the swastika and the meander. The spiral disappears. Sometimes he resorts to animal or human figures, but even then only to reproduce them in ideogrammatic form. He arranges his highly ornamented motifs in parallel bands. Archaeologists distinguish a transitional period, which they name the protogeometric, preceding the geometric proper.

Vase shapes are still inspired by those of the Sub-Mycenaean period, but have been adapted to primitive and utilitarian requirements. Their purpose is to act as containers for liquids: the amphora for carrying, the oenochoe for pouring wine, the krater for mixing, the cup, which has a border and relatively tall stem and is sometimes described as a "tea-cup"

The decoration is adapted to the structure and to enhancing the value of the shape. Until the end of the ninth century it remains in the non-figurative field. The motifs—drawn free hand or, a little later, traced with a compass—are simplified to an extreme degree: circles and concentric semicircles, hatched triangles, lozenges, acute

27

zigzags, traced in black on the natural colour of the clay, distributed as a general rule over a central zone, while the rest of the vase is merely glazed. In studying these vases one is struck by the sensibility of the craftsmen who created them. Balanced proportions, sober distribution of the motifs, the creation of a varied and contrasted rhythm all served to lend significance to the space in which the agile hand of the potter did its work.

As life became easier, commercial interchange increased. The other peoples in Greece were quick to recognise the superiority of Athens, judging by the numerous traces uncovered in Thessaly, the Phocis, the Peloponnese, the Cyclades and even Asia Minor.

This supremacy is confirmed during the course of the ninth and eight centuries, when the Attic style reaches maturity. A surer grasp of technique permits a greater variety of shapes. The cup becomes shallower, resting with ease on a larger base. The oenochoe acquires a distinct profile, while the neck of the amphora grows longer and is given two simple vertical handles. The repertory of decoration, discarding the curve and circles, emphasises the straight line and its multiple combinations, resulting in the "Greek" patterns characteristic of this style. The tiered zones of varying size increase in number, encroach on the whole vase and punctuate the surface with a regular rhythm without giving prominence to any particular element in the decoration.

The social transformations which mark the end of the ninth and the beginning of the eight century have their repercussions on art. Religious beliefs change, cremation is replaced by burial. This very novel conception of life and death inevitably brings about a change in the artist's vision. Just as the Creto-Mycenaean kings flattered themselves with reproductions of their deeds and actions on their palace walls, so too did the eupatrides of Athens like to have scenes of their lives and of the splendid ceremonies accompanying their passage into the beyond illustrated on their funerary monuments.

The finest examples of the vases typical of this period come from the Kerameikos cemetery* close to Dipylon* Gate. The most usual forms are the amphora with double-hooped handles and the open-mouthed krater with a truncated conical foot, which was deposited in the grave. The base is often pierced so that the dead man may have his share of the libations, milk or honey, water or wine. The decoration unfurls in friezes* placed one above the other and covering the whole surface of the vase; one or two zones, usually between the two handles, are reserved for scenes showing human or animal figures.

The most interesting vases are those with human figures. In addition to their artistic value, the themes employed—naval battles, bodies lying in state and funeral processions—are precious testimony to the life and beliefs of Athenians at this period. If Attica took no part in the colonising movement of the eight and seventh centuries, Attic mariners were engaged in coast-wise traffic and knew how to defend their shores against pirates. Thus the decoration on Dipylon vases often recalls engagements in

which the wealthy ship-owners took part. Long rows of oarsmen, drenched and buffetted by the waves, scenes of rapine, warriors in combat: in vivid pictures such as these we have a perpetual memorial of their ceaseless conflicts. Funeral rites are another frequent subject. The dead man lies on his ceremonial bier, surrounded by groups of relatives and mourning women who weep and tear their hair.

The vision to which these primitive artists bear witness, very close to our modern aesthetic sense, is significant. They pass quite naturally from the abstract drawing of ornamental motifs to a semantic of the human figure, in which certain geometrical signs are combined to reproduce a figurative image: a circle (the head) placed above a triangle (the body), a trapezoid (the arms raised above the head in sign of mourning), parallel forks (the feet). The simplification and paring down of the drawing, in alliance with the geometrism of the decoration, underlines the purely conceptual nature of the answer to the problems posed. A pair of horses drawing a chariot is presented as a single body with two heads and eight legs. To show the forward movement, the legs and feet are drawn in profile, unlike the bust and arms which are frontal.

Attic products are not confined to these vases of monumental dimensions. Vessels needed for daily life are also found, amphorae, oenochoiai, pyxides, all pots in current use.

29

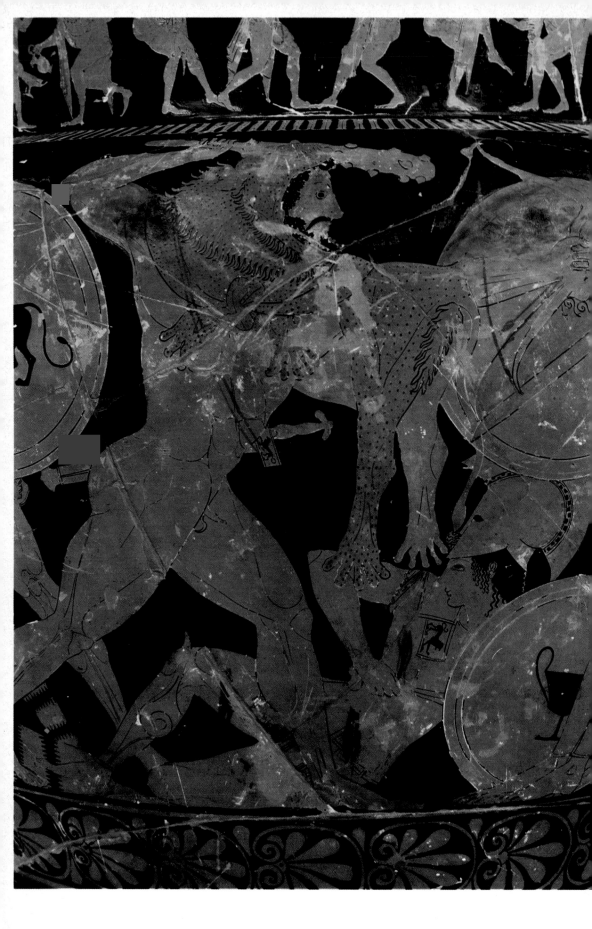

Krater by Euphronios (detail)
Herakles in combat with Geryon
About 520 B.C.
Museum at Arezzo

Colour in Greek art

It is virtually impossible to define the role of colour in Greek art, since the major painting and chief painted monuments, which alone could furnish the elements of appraisal indispensable in forming a judgment, have disappeared. All that we have to fill the gap, in however small a way, are observations in the writings of the travellers* and of other authors of the first century B.C., who were able to admire these works at first hand.

These texts are supplemented by a number of more or less faithful copies and somewhat free interpretations of the original works: vase paintings, mosaics, the decoration to Roman houses. However, there is a kind of osmosis between major painting and the minor arts, which makes the work of the potters a fairly faithful reflection of the chromatic characteristics of monumental painting.

Colour was of prime importance. Colour was the complementary element in sculpture and architecture, which it came to enrich. But why did the Greeks assign it so great a place?

The causes go deep. The climate and the quality of the light are two factors which undoubtedly influenced Greek art. The sky is limpid, there is the sun, the hues of the landscape are diluted, almost robbed of colour and act like a transparent curtain, animated by vibrations, against which the graphic outline of the contours becomes detached and acquires a primordial significance. If to this natural factor one adds another unavoidable influence, the inborn taste for ornament found among peoples of the Middle East, it will be seen why the Greeks were led to experiment with colour, such a pleasing, sensual element, and to incorporate it in their architecture and statuary. The values of marble, stone, wood, or of a wall were enhanced by enrichment throught the addition of colour. Today it is difficult to grasp the guiding principles which led architects to such a wide and various use of colour in their buildings. Time and men have spared few of the treasures of Greek painting.

In this atmosphere where light effaces detail to the benefit of line, the chromatic element, adapting itself to the landscape, had to serve as a "bridge" to offset and tone down, by a subtle interplay, the over-harsh precision of the contours. In the landscape, therefore, shape was identified as a coherent whole. The work of man was modelled on nature and integrated with it. The use of colour was often dictated by practical considerations. Colour-washing, for example, is still quite frequently employed in many Greek villages to reduce the resonance of walls, which suggests that the same motives may have impelled the ancient Hellenes to paint their monumental buildings and houses.

There was bound to be a degree of disorder in the huge temple agglomerations, since the whim of the builders had produced a successive accumulation of structures in varying styles and materials. Statues of all sizes were scattered among them indiscriminately. Everywhere he went, the passer-by had his eye caught by a riot of

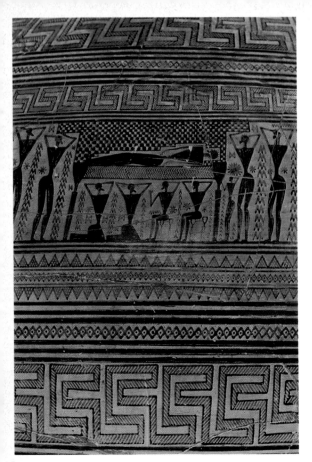

colour, whether from the religious sanctuaries just mentioned, the civic buildings—stoa,* bouleuterion,* prytaneum*—or again from the houses of the wealthy, with their courtyards surrounded by porticos whose wall-bases and columns were painted.

But major architecture was not alone in benefiting from colour, which was applied also to smaller structures and indeed even to objects such as the tripods carried aloft by the choragoi.* Neither should we forget the reliefs which lined an entire street on the southern slopes of the Acropolis,* nor again the funerary stelae, sculpted and painted in illustration of the cult of the dead, which surmounted the tombs normally to be found at the city gateways.

In his guide, Pausanias describes the mural paintings still extant at Athens at the end of the second century A.D.: the paintings in the temples of Theseus and the Dioscuri and in the porticoes of the Poikile Stoa. We know too that the best works of Polygnotos were still to be seen in the Cnidian lesche* at Delphi. There are numerous references to the presence of mural decorations in public buildings, palaces—for example the palace of King Archelaos* of Macedon, decorated by Zeuxis—or private houses, such as the house of Alcibiades* at Athens on which Agatharcos had worked.

Until the end of the fifth century the artist treats colour as a decorator. Although we possess not a single work painted by the masters of this period, Polygnotos, Mikon,* Panainos,* Parrhasios,* Zeuxis, we learn from the written authorities that their palette was very limited. Pliny remarks on the colours white, black, yellow and red used in Greek painting, but some archaic paintings in a brilliant blue have been discovered. The artists were ignorant of both the third dimension and chiaroscuro and merely filled in the outline of their drawings with flat tints.

In all probability polychromy and complementary colours were already being used in the fourth century B.C., but it was only later, in the Hellenistic period, which has been called the "*grand siècle*" of Greek painting, that its use was perfected and the transition effected from this painting on a single plane to one which evokes three-dimensional space. As evidence we can point to the "battle of Issos" mosaic, probably a copy of a mural painting.

Archaic art

According to Pliny, the Egyptians claimed to have passed the art of painting on to the Greeks, while the Greeks declared that its origins were to be sought at Sikyon* or Corinth. It is clear that even in archaic times these two Peloponnesian cities were already important artistic centres. The first schools had already been formed there and mural painting was no doubt practised.

Most of the vases from these districts imitate the style of frescoes. An Argive krater is eloquent illustration of the freedom this inspired, the spatial conception which gives one the feeling of looking not at a potter's simple decoration but at a monumental painting. Several of the artists who contributed to the progressive revival of this art and the invention of new processes are known to us by name. Pliny cites Kleanthes of Corinth* who was the first to adopt line drawing, a technique hitherto reserved for major painting; he also mentions Kleanthes' imitators, Aridikes of Corinth* and Telephanes of Sikyon* who practised it by underlining details with colour. Later there was Ekphantes of Corinth,* the first to use a reddish tint derived from ground potsherds and Kraton of Sikyon, who silhouetted black figures on a white ground.

Strabo also adds his testimony and speaks admiringly of two compositions which adorned a sanctuary close to Olympia,* the "Capture of Troy" by Kleanthes of Corinth and "Artemis riding an eagle" by Arigontos. Pliny also tells us that Greek painters worked in Etruria and Latium, at Ardea and Lanurio. If his information is to be believed, it seems that these pictures consisted only of line figure drawings filled in with a single colour, with no foreshortening or chiaroscuro.

Vases apart, there are few original witnesses to give us an idea of what monumental archaic art was like. Plaques of painted earthenware have been discovered at Themos* and at Kalydon in Aetolia. They acted as metopes in adorning wooden temples of the seventh century. They are badly damaged and of provincial manufacture, some years later than the famous Corinthian oenochoe. Their treatment provides valuable information about the technique employed at this period. The surface has been coated with a yellow slip from which one or more polychrome figures stand out, and also some decorative motifs.

Six of these metopes have come down to us in a fair state of preservation. Some of the subjects are mythological, Perseus in flight after killing the Medusa, Procne and

33

Ionian amphora
Detail of masculine bust
About 540-530
Paris, Louvre
▼

Painted metope from the temple of **Thermi** ▶
Corinthian style
Second half of the 7th century B.C.
Athens, National Museum

Philomela dismembering the body of Itys, but there are various other themes, a hunts-
man returning with game, people in conversation.

   Some small clay votive tablets dating from the end of the seventh century have
also been recovered from the temple of Poseidon at Pentescouphia near Corinth.
These were ex-voto tablets offered by common people to the gods to solicit their help.
Naive in treatment, they are the work of potter-painters such as Timonides* and shed
useful light on the daily life of the time.

   Other plaques of the same type have been discovered in Attica. From the
technical point of view, they differ scarcely at all from the vases. However, two from
the Acropolis provide rare examples of free painting. Larger and thicker than the
preceding tablets, in a style approaching that of Euthymides,* they are different in
colouring and delicate in character and like the Thermos metopes must have served
some architectural purpose.

From Corinth we have the only examples of painting on wood to come from Greece, panels discovered thirty years ago in a cave near Pitsa.* What makes them different from vase painting is their spirited quality, simplicity in composition, richness of colouring and the freedom of the drawing.

Another important artistic centre was Ionia, where monumental painting of historical subjects was a feature. According to tradition, Saurias of Samos* was the first to draw the shadow cast by a horse in the sun. Again, Pausanias tells us that Kalliphon of Samos* had painted for the temple of Artemis at Ephesus the battle between the Greeks and the Trojans before the burning of the fleet which is celebrated in the Iliad. Herodotus* tells us that the architect Mandrokles* had a painting made for the Heraion at Samos showing the bridge he built over the Bosporos in 513, with the army filing past Darius,* seated upon his throne.

These themes will be taken up again by the decorators of the great sarcophagi at Clazomenai and probably sum up the repertory of Ionian painters of this period.

But these glowing literary accounts are insufficient to allow of a critical appraisal of ancient aesthetic and of the pictorial style of Antiquity. In compensation, a methodical study of the written sources, combined with what we know of the work of the potter-painters, goes some way towards filling the gap.

For two centuries (the seventh and the sixth) the influence of the archaic art which succeeded the geometric is felt over almost the whole of the Hellenic world, from Ionia to mainland Greece, from the Aegean islands to Italy.

The craftsmen of preceding centuries had adopted the schematic procedures common to primitive civilisations: geometrism, stylisation of forms. Later, in the light of experience, they draw increasingly closer to nature.

At the close of the eight century, under Oriental influence, geometrism is on the wane. At first the hatchings, swastikas and spirals persist, mingled with new additions. The urge to decorate and the "horror vacui" still predominate and the human figure, difficult to interpret, will only start to play an important role towards the end of the seventh century. Gods and heroes follow on the heels of man, relegating zoomorphic or purely decorative ornament to second place. The Asiatic world, from now on, is being supplanted by the ideal of Greek humanism. Painting becomes narrative. This evolution comes to completion in the course of the sixth century with the adoption of the black-figured style. Henceforth the human figure will dominate and one sees it growing and developing, encroaching on all parts of the vase, until one or two figures occupy the entire surface. These changes were not unopposed. Towards the middle of the sixth century two schools confront one another: the "traditionalists", faithful to the practice of division into zones with plant or animal ornament, who conserve the grace and pictorial qualities of Ionian art; and the "innovators", champions of the new trends towards simplification and unity of composition, influenced furthermore by the impressive solemnity of sculptural works, and open to the Doric ideal of austere nobility.

The Greek world and the Orient

The seventh century appears in a new perspective once the culmination is reached of the great colonising movement which began towards the middle of the eighth century. Little by little the colonies gain their freedom, alter their trading patterns and adapt their products to suit the taste of their new clientele. To beat their competitors, craftsmen must cultivate variety and novelty. Their success impels the mother-states to follow their example, and imported wares (gems, chased weapons, inlaid ivories, embroidered or woven stuffs) captivate the imagination and provide a stimulus to new expression: Greek ivories and bronzes of the period will soon be covered with scenes of oriental inspiration.

The same influence, less directly mediated, is seen in vase painting. Local tradition persists, but adapts to itself in individual style motifs and themes from the repertory of eastern countries. The wild beasts dear to Syria and Egypt—lions, panthers, birds, monsters, gryphons, sphinxes, chimeras, sirens—make their appearance. Towards the year 700 this wave of orientalism is beginning to penetrate nearly every part of the Greek world.

By the sixth century the cities of Asia Minor, Phocaea,* Clazomenai, Ephesus, Miletus,* have become economic, intellectual and artistic centres of Greek life. Equally there are numerous and thriving workshops in the Ionian colonies of Egypt, Italy, Etruria and indeed on the neighbouring islands, such as Rhodes and Crete.

In contrast with "Doric" severity, the Ionic movement, permeated by reminiscences of Asia, displays a pronounced taste for the monstrous, for picturesque narrative and sumptuous decoration, to which it brings finesse and sensitivity.

The Rhodian vases rank among the finest creations of this period. Close to the shores of Asia, the potters of Rhodes had had opportunity to admire the gorgeous carpets, embroidered tissues and inlaid coffers brought back by their mariners and were skilful enough to use them as the basis of newly-inspired decorations.

The necropolis at Camiras has yielded wine containers resembling in shape vases in metal and whose decoration recalls the vases of Susiane.*

During the second half of the sixth century a new style appears, that of Fikellura,* a cemetery close to Camiros. Works in this style are also to be found at Samos, Miletus and even in the Nile delta. The tendency is towards greater lightness, more space between the figures and less use of decorative motifs.

Other insular schools must also have been making many experiments, in particular those of Crete, which played an important role in introducing new oriental forms and techniques destined for a great future in Greece. Thus we find Cretan potters transposing the shapes of metal vases to clay and rendering certain of the details in relief. We observe, too, that the Cretans were the first to apply to ceramic the process in metal decoration by which an incision is made with a chisel, and that they combined it with silhouette and line drawing; this technique was later widely used at Corinth.

37

Again, this time probably under Cypriot inspiration, the Cretans adopted a wider and richer range of colour, delicate shades of yellow and blue being harmonised with the traditional red, white and black. However, although the repercussion of these innovations carried further than one might expect, this period of artistic fermentation in the Cretan school was relatively short-lived.

The settlement of Greek colonists in the city of Naukratis,* enlarged by Ahmes in 570, is a further stimulus to exchanges. Following Egyptian example, an important place is reserved in sculpture, as in painting, for the human figure. The diffusion of the epic poems encourages painters to break away from the narrow limitations of the geometric style, by the use of realism in their pictures and by illustration of myths. Thus scenes representing the judgment of Paris or one of the Danaides after the beheading of her husband, a subject familiar in Egypt, have been recognised on vase fragments.

Clazomenai on the gulf of Smyrna* is famous above all for the sarcophagi which came from its workshops. Even so, most of the vases found along the coast and

38

Rhodian oenochoe, the "Levi oenochoe"
Animal zones
7th century B.C.

in Aeolis seem to have come from there, judging by the fairly close similarity of their technique and ornament to those of the sarcophagi. The most frequent shapes are the slender amphora, the trefoil-mouthed oenochoe and the plate. The subjects are silhouetted in black, picked up in red, with numerous touches of white on the clay ground.

The preoccupation is still with decoration, the artist aiming at an over-all effect, but from now on the human figure acquires a precise mythological significance.

The Ionian dinoi and Northampton amphorae have affinity with Clazomenai pottery and typify the mingling of Ionic and Attic features.

Some thirty hydriai (water pots) from the Etruscan necropolis of Cerveteri* date from 540-520 B.C. They are all alike, heavy and rustic, and despite their affinity with the middle pottery of Ionia attract attention by their original style. The subjects are treated with a sense of humour which verges often on ridicule. An acute observer of everyday reality, the author debunks the exploits of gods and heroes by his malicious and ingenious caricatures. The *chef-d'oeuvre* of the series shows Herakles grappling with the myrmidons of the Egyptian king Busiris, whose habit was to sacrifice all foreigners to Zeus. The hero, with his giant's body and little boy demeanour, is held up to ridicule. What is more, the same disrespect will also be shown towards the king of the gods, Hephaistos the lame, or Apollo.

In addition to his verve and humour, the artist possesses a very highly developed feeling for colour, exploiting to the full the very limited range at his disposal.

These hydriai are probably parodies of Ionian or Egyptian mural paintings. There is evidence that a celebrated school of painting existed in Ionia during the sixth century, and the hydriai may well reflect its spirit.

The Chalcidian vases date from the second half of the sixth century. They are the products of various workshops of Euboea* or its Italian colonies, in particular Cumae. This group of vases is remarkable for the extraordinary lustre of the black glaze with bluish reflections and the large use made of incision. The decoration unfurls in parallel bands, the centre band being reserved for human figures, the others for floral ornament of oriental origin. The compositions, all of mythological inspiration and treated in a spirit which recalls the Homeric poems, are ordered symmetrically and animated by a pronounced movement. The shapes—kraters, hydriai, amphorae— are quite clearly derived from metal vases.

Laconian pottery is the product of both Cyrene and Sparta, at that time in continuous contact with Ionia. In the seventh century it is influenced by Corinth, in the sixth by Athens. Especially noteworthy are the kylikes, in which the painting covers all the interior of the cup, often bordered by a fine edging of stylised pomegranates, much-favoured by the overseas clientele. In all likelihood they reproduce scenes taken from panel or wall paintings. The cup portraying king Arkesilas II of Cyrene is justly famous. The arrangement of the scene, the importance given to the figure of the ruler, prove that the author was inspired by Egyptian funerary reliefs.

Corinthian oenochoe, the "Chigi oenochoe"
Line of warriors (detail)
Third quarter of the 7th century B.C.
Rome, Villa Guilia

Ionian cup, the "Bird-catcher" cup
Man in a forest
About 530-520 B.C.
Paris, Louvre

Corinth, a city with a large population and a relatively evolved political and economic structure, was a great coloniser even before Athens, and a commercial centre whose influence extended over the whole Aegean. Syracuse* was founded from Corinth in 733. Corinthian ships plied the Mediterranean in every direction, from the Black Sea* to Sicily. Corinth was a necessary staging-post between East and West, the Orient figured largely in her trading life and exerted a notable influence over the evolution of her art. Her craftsmen worked for export. They made a speciality of the little pots for perfumed oil, intended primarily for athletes, and for a time had a monopoly of them. Vases of large dimensions will be found only at a later period, in the sixth century, when the need to beat Athens on her own ground forces Corinthian potters to imitate their rivals' technique.

The first half of the seventh century, a time when Attic painting is still in the experimental stage, sees Corinth at its height. The vase shapes which enjoy the greatest vogue are the aryballos and the alabastron. The former, Cypriot in origin, is an elongated sphere with a narrow neck and flat mouth; initially pot-bellied, it later becomes first ovoid and then pear-shaped. The alabastron, copied from Egyptian prototypes, appears towards the middle of the seventh century and seems to have inspired a new vase shape, the olpe. The style of these pots passes through a number of phases. To begin with there is a marked oriental influence. Linear decoration alternates with friezes of animals, which in time become less numerous, ending with isolated figures. The apogee is reached towards the middle of the seventh century, with a series of vases whose mouth is formed by an animal or human head. Miniature ornamentation attains a high degree of perfection, a fully decorative effect, and has rightly been characterised a "magnificent style". The most beautiful known example is the Chigi oenochoe, so-called from the name of its first owner. The decoration, arranged in friezes, illustrates scenes from daily life, lion or fox hunts, the judgment of Paris, which is found here for the first time, or battle episodes.

Protocorinthian is significant above all for its perfection, during the first half of the seventh century, of the "black-figured" style, typical of the whole archaic period. The "magnificent style" was of short duration. Its disappearance is probably due to economic factors, the execution of such minute detail being too demanding of time and labour. During the last third of the seventh century, as demand increases, production becomes industrialised. The human figure disappears, there is a return to oriental decorative motifs—confronted sphinxes, panthers, lions, anthropomorphic monsters. The secondary filling-in elements fulfil the same role as the principal figures.

Following on the decline of Protocorinthian, the following century ushers in a new era. Corinthian pottery is now at its most expansive and its products flood the ancient world. The commercial rivalry between Athens and Corinth explains their artistic development. Up to this time each has been serving a different clientele, Athens working for a local market, Corinth for export. From the beginning of the sixth century the situation alters. The beneficent laws of Solon* act as a stimulus to

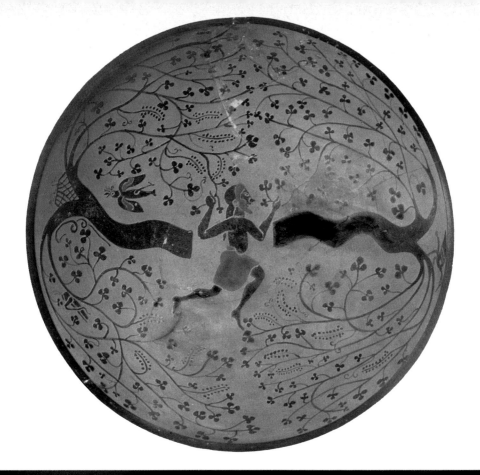

Corinthian krater (detail)
Banquet of Herakles and Eurytios
About 600 B.C.
Paris, Louvre

Athenian commerce, and its traffic now extends to parts of the Aegean and Magna Graeca which until now were the undisputed domain of Corinth. No longer sure of their own ground, the Corinthians resort to outright imitation of Attic products. In addition to the traditional perfume pots, they launch on the market column kraters intended to supplant those of their rivals. The borrowings, moreover, are mutual, as the Athenians in their turn imitate both Corinthian motifs and vase shapes.

Towards the middle of the sixth century the extraordinary drive and expansion of Attica force Corinth to abandon the struggle. However, with improvements in casting, this city of bronzesmiths has a chance to concentrate on other products, just as lucrative but less vulnerable to competition.

The motifs undergo a change. The geometric rigour of the seventh century is toned down, the borrowings of oriental trend are transformed, in a way which allows scope for Hellenic humanism. The animal style, still bearing marks of the Orient, is succeeded by narrative decoration, in which the subjects are taken from everyday life.

From the second quarter of the sixth century, to compete with Athens, the traditional subjects of banquets and dances are replaced by legends and myths. A fine example is provided by the amphora which depicts the murder of Ismene by Tydeus. The dramatic character of the composition suggests Attic influence, also perhaps indicated by the reddish slip which simulates the Attic coating. A krater now in Berlin illustrates the Amphiaraos* legend. The scene shows him setting out for the plain of Thebes, where he is to meet his death. The other side of the vase bears a painting of the races at the funeral games held in honour of Pelias, an episode from the Argonaut cycle. According to Pausanias, the same composition figured on a coffer dedicated at Olympia by Kypselos, tyrant of Corinth. One can therefore conclude that these two presentations were inspired by a common source, a Corinthian mural painting. In any case, we know that the city continued to be an important centre of painting even after the fabrication of vases ceased. It was near Sikyon that the only panel paintings on wood dating from this epoch, as also some small altars in decorated terra cotta, were discovered.

Proto-Attic pottery

The black figured technique may have been invented at Corinth, but its fullest development takes place at Athens, where it becomes one of the characteristic features of archaic Attic art. Even twenty years ago, the absence of documents led scholars to believe that a long gap supervened between the production of the geometric period and that of the sixth century vases. Since then, numerous finds have revealed the existence of an intermediary period, in a style strongly influenced by the East, which has been christened proto-attic; it shows a logical development of the innovations of late geometric.

The huge Diplyon jars have disappeared, to be replaced by other, more elegant, funerary vessels, the loutrophoroi; hydriai act as water pourers, pot-bellied amphorae as wine containers, kraters for mixing wine, while the kotyle, a deep cup with handles, is used for drinking.

The evolution of the decoration provides an even better guide to this period of transition. The first phase of the transformation is illustrated by a hydria found at Analatos close to Athens, where memories of the geometric period are combined with certain motifs of orientalising trend, making their first appearance in Attic art.

The painters of the following generation strike us as being more emancipated from the geometric tradition. They resort frequently to incision, coat human bodies with white paint, abandon tiered zones and show that concentration on people which is a hall-mark of the Athenian ideal in art.

This evolution finds completion in the second half of the century, during which line drawing is replaced by silhouette and the proto-attic evolves towards the black-figured style. The vases continue to be of monumental dimensions, the depiction of scenes, often mythological, leads to a reduction of in-filling ornament, the action becomes more animated and dramatic, the technique more assured. The Nessos amphora demonstrates that Attic pottery is by now fully in command of its expressive media.

Attic pottery

In the sixth century, thanks to some enlightened and audacious statesmen, Attica becomes a powerful commercial centre. Economic prosperity gives new life to the arts and to literature. Athens acquires new temples and other buildings, covered with frescoes and populated with sculptures. Enriched and fortified, the city is poised for the conquest of new markets and the full assertion of her supremacy. Craftsmen, writers and traders flock to Athenian territory from all sides, encouraged by the laws of Solon which favour the settlement of foreigners in the city. This is the setting in which one of the most interesting of all periods of painting will have its flowering.

By the first decades of the century, the Athenian workshops and potters are already declaring their mastery. Corinthian artists settle in Athens, contributing by their experience and the novel elements they bring with them to the transformation in style. We shall trace this evolution through the work of potters and painters whose names are known to us, since for the first time at Athens they are now signing their work. "Sophilos me grapsen" ("Sophilos painted me") runs the signature on a dinos fragment found at Pharsalus, and this is the first name whose identification is at all certain. There follows, which is very rare, an inscription describing the subject: "Funeral games in honour of Patroklus". Is the artist consciously imitating the fresco painters who signed and sometimes even gave a title to their work? His technique seems to confirm that this is so. In other examples of his work he actually uses the method adopted in free painting, placing the white for the flesh directly on the clay instead of applying it to the black medium.

The demands of an ever-widening market had to be met, which means that utilitarian products preponderate, although there is no lack of quality pottery. Furthermore, so eager were Athenian workshops to get the better of their Corinthian rivals that they did not scruple to steal their motifs. Ornamental bands, palmettes,

lotus flowers, fawns, sphinxes make their appearance, combined with typically Attic elements.

If the first quarter of the sixth century bears the imprint of Solon and his impressive personality, the advent of Peisistratos* leaves its mark on the destinies of the city for the remainder of the century. Under the rule of the tyrant, Athenian pottery enjoys an extraordinary renaissance which goes hand in hand with the blossoming of the other arts.

The glory of this period is a piece of quite outstanding quality known as the "François vase", signed by Ergotimos the potter and Kleitias the painter. This vase has been described as a "Bible of Antiquity", on account of the richness and variety of its themes, arranged in six superimposed rows and containing 200 people and animals and 128 inscriptions. The chiselled drawing, sure and precise, reveals a certain mastery, while the attitudes are much less conventional than in the past. One still detects a certain archaic stiffness—an eye full-face in a profile head, angular contours —suggesting that the artist is not yet in command of his technique. But a breath of life is already stirring among these compositions, which probably attracted a rich Etruscan purchaser.

This vase is treated in miniature, a fact all the more surprising since this is the time of a developing monumental tradition, coming close to major painting.

The second half of the sixth century, when the Peisistratides were ruling, is remarkable for an event of signal importance: the sudden cessation of Corinthian production, which leaves the field free for the Athenians. They have no need to fear competition from the workshops of the Cyclades, Rhodes and Miletus, and dominate the market unchallenged. Their vases are of finer quality and more impervious, the variety and richness of their human figuring is more congenial to the new aesthetic sense of the clientele, sated by the floral and animal ornamentation which still commands the loyalty of the insular potters.

The third quarter of the sixth century is one of the happiest periods for black-figured pottery. The decorative style is replaced by narrative, in which the painter allows his imagination free rein, relating heroic legends in the manner of the poets of the epics, elegies and dithyrambics,* depicting the Panathenian festivals, or the festivals of Dionysos, dedicated to the new cult of the god of wine and pleasure, which from the time of Peisistratos enjoyed the freedom of the city. In one sense this school, which pays heed to grandeur and nobility and seeks to unify its compositions by magnifying the persons and placing them in hieratic attitudes, is a faithful continuation of the severity of the Doric ideal. There is also another, concurrent, school which retains the pictorialism, mannerism, preciosity and refinement of Ionian art.

Refugees from Asia Minor, fleeing their homeland in face of wars and revolutions, bring with them a taste for pleasure and the easy life very welcome to the tyrant, anxious as he is to provide diversions for both common people and nobility, whose reluctance to support a regime of oppression he knows only too well.

It is thus not surprising that between 550 and 530 a particular form of cup known as that of "the Little Masters" enjoys great favour in Attica and all the lands oversea. With its thin walls and tall stem it is of surpassing elegance; the cup is characterised by a flat swelling basin whose exterior rims carry discreet decoration in the form of small isolated figures—animals, female heads, horsemen—and which bear a signature or some cheerful inscription, for example, "greetings, have a drink".

The two dominant personalities of the period are Exekias and Amasis. The first signed as both painter and potter, giving greater importance to shape than to decoration. His known works are not numerous, but his influence was considerable. He reshapes the amphora, giving it a double continuous curve in place of the neck clearly distinct from the belly. He paints the interior of cups, a bold innovation destined to meet with great success, and raises the simple happenings of daily life to the austere heights of heroic emotion, thus anticipating classical tragedy.

Judging by his name, Amasis was of Egyptian origin. He signs as a potter, but was probably painter as well. His great merit lies in his elegant and well-proportioned shapes, he delights in elaborate detail, decorative but attractive. On his many amphorae, cups and lekythoi he shows us festive gatherings, dionysiac dances, scenes from mythology.

◄ Corinthian aryballos
Winged spirit running
End of 7th century B.C.
Paris, Louvre

Attic krater, the "François vase" (detail)
Chariot of Zeus
About 575 B.C.
Florence, archaeological museum
▼

The black-figured technique appears to have reached its peak with Exekias, an exceptional master and one of the greatest of all potter-painters. At this period, the archaic masters have acquired full command of their means of expression and can render their vision and ideas to perfection.

But in the last quarter of the sixth century there is a change of spirit and feeling, the old methods reveal themselves as an inadequate medium for translating the new preoccupations of the Greek world.

Between 540 and 530 a new invention, outwardly very simple, initiates a genuine revolution in the technique of painting. Formerly the figures and decorative details had been silhouetted in black glaze on the natural surface of the clay. The new technique reverses the process, reserving the red colour of the clay for the figures, set off by a ground uniformly black. This allowed for greater freedom of movement, since a line made by drawing can be more supple than one made by incision.

This change was certainly not due to chance, but to a constellation of factors connected with the evolution of the artistic ideal and the need to express it through

51

"Chalcidian" amphora (detail)
Theseus and the Minotaur: satyrs
End of sixth century B.C.
Paris, Louvre

appropriate means. Until the end of the sixth century the artist's view of the work is conventional. But as this vision rids itself of abstract formulae, man comes to assert himself as he really is. The sculptor and painter are at pains to represent him in his mortal aspects, they describe his anatomy and the volatile play of his feelings and attitudes. It is thus natural that this new method, very close to monumental painting, should have met with a ready response from the artists. All the evidence suggests that the black-figured technique lingered on for several more decades. It even survived until as late as the end of the fourth century on the large amphorae containing oil which were presented to victors in the Panathenian games. But from now on it will be applied only to a mass production, whose quality leaves much to be desired.

The time between the end of archaism and the beginning of classical art is occupied by an intermediate period, ranging in duration from 50 to 60 years and filled with tragic events. It coincides with the death of Peisistratos, the rule of his sons Hipparchos* and Hippias,* the early days of Athenian democracy, the Ionian revolt and the Persian wars; a troubled time in which settled ways are overturned and self-control and austerity demanded of the citizens. The gaiety of archaic, an import from the East, gives way to "severity", harbinger of the classical revolution.

The new style is indicative of this spirit. Its subject, to the exclusion of all else, is the human being, whose daily life, occupations and amusements are recounted with meticulous accuracy. The isolated human countenance is studied for its own sake, and as the hand becomes more skilful, thanks to the new technique which permits greater liberties, the drawing improves, foreshortening is employed, the law of frontality is broken. From now on the painter can articulate the anatomy of his bodies, and vary the stance of his people, presenting them full face, in profile or three-quarters. Under the influence of monumental painting, with the assistance of hatchings he tries to render the plasticity of objects and people by modelling.

All these triumphs are the result of much groping and laborious investigation. The work of the earliest artists is tentative, full of errors. To begin with their drawing remains as unsubtle as that applied to black-figure, which they still continue to use. This is so in the case of the "Andokides Painter"*—an unknown artist working on behalf of the potter Andokides or in his workshop—who has been credited with the merit of inventing the new method. Stylistically he shows affinity with Exekias, and the archaic mannerism of the engraver comes out in the details, the stiffness of the gestures and the scheme of composition. On some vases he makes use of both techniques, treating one face in red-figure, the other in black-figure. It has also been noticed that the paintings of this master stand in a very exact relationship to the reliefs of the Treasury at Siphnos dating from around 525 B.C. This shows that the painting of this period evolves in parallel with the sculpture and is often influenced by it.

In fact the credit for fathering the new form should go to the "Menon Painter", identified some years ago under the name of Psiax. He was the first to free himself from decorativism and to treat the shape as a contour in its own right and no longer as the

53

product of internal details. Using both techniques, he paints small vases and cups. He was also one of the forerunners in the presentation of human figures viewed three-quarters.

The activity of Epiktetos, one of the most illustrious masters of this time, belongs to the years between 520 and 480, or thereabouts. He too worked on cups and plates, vessels well-suited to meet his preference for isolated figures treated in miniature. His drawing is exact and supple. He follows the body's inflections with meticulous care, expressing its masses by means of the contours alone, which he adapts to a surface decoration, careful to secure a good rhythm of composition, underlined by the contrasted effects of hot red on the black ground. Discarding mythological subjects, he applies himself to the current scene, to the life of the people in its broadly comic, Aristophanic, aspects, a genre which culminates in the ribaldries of Brygos.* This last painter describes the habits of the gilded youth of his day, their orgies, their athletic sports, and delights in drawing the beautiful bodies of the ephebi—he is their recognised painter—as he admired them in the palaestra.

Other minor masters worked in the same genre of cup painting. It is not, however, until we reach the time of Leagros, which covers the last decade of the sixth century, that we find artists trying out a new style, for example Kimon of Kleonai* in major painting. Like the sculptors, the painters and potters attempt something new by breaking the stiffness of the stylisation. But although this enriched their modes of expression, there was still no success in the interpretation of three-dimensional space. It is in this direction that Euphronios,* Euthymides and Phintias* lead the way.

Euphronios must have enjoyed a very great reputation since his rival Euthymides, in an inscription traced on one of his amphorae, boasts of having surpassed him: "Euphronios never did anything like this". At first he seems to have worked in the service of master potters. But after the Persian wars, when prosperity brought into existence a new clientele, he set up on his own. Like his predecessors, he takes pleasure in genre scenes—athletic exercises, horsemen, young men setting out for battle, feasting

54

Corinthian hydria
Dirge for Achilles
Middle 6th century B.C.
Paris, Louvre

courtesans—but his feeling for the monumental prompts him to draw compositions of more elevated character, in which he returns to mythological subjects, deployed with assurance over the major part of the vase.

Euthymides' rival Euphronios is one of the most characteristic artists of the severe style. His people, usually planted in groups of three which gives an effect of mass, occupy almost the entire vase. His compositions reveal a remarkable talent for observation. Master of his media, he can now convey the torsion of a body or the volume of muscles. Like many of his contemporaries, Euthymides pays greater attention to Theseus, the Athenian hero *par excellence*, than to the Peloponnesian Herakles.

The disturbances of the war do not appear to have hindered in any noticeable way the activity of the workshops at Kerameikos. Quite the contrary, this period, continuously fertile in experiment, marks the end of archaism and the birth of a new world: the classical world, prelude of European civilisation.

In this first quarter of the fifth century there is great activity among the cup painters. Two of these are justly famous, Douris* and the Brygos painter.

There are a number of works bearing the signature of Douris, and in addition he has been credited with a large quantity of unsigned pieces (about two hundred). At times his art has an emotive quality. This is so with the painting of Eos bearing away the corpse of her son Memnon, an unaccustomed scene from the Trojan epic cycle, highly favoured by popular tradition, in which some critics have seen "the poignant emotion of a Pieta, conceived by a pagan painter".

The personality of the "Brygos painter" is much more strongly marked. With him, new interests become evident. He aims at dramatic new effects achieved by highlights in white, red or yellow. He uses gilding to render the brilliance of weapons and jewelry and hatched modelling to give volume to bodies. He is more skilful than his predecessors in conveying the contrast between light and shadows. He is the author of large mythological or epic compositions, for example his "Sack of Troy"   55

Ionian hydria, "Caeretan"
Europa and the Bull
About 540-520 B.C.
Rome, Villa Giulia

Krater by Euphronios
Herakles in combat with Geryon
Dances and diversions
About 520 B.C.
Museum at Arezzo

whose febrile emotion successfully evokes the tragic events of that famous night.

Makron, an employee of the potter Hieron,* is fond of painting frenzied Maenad dances, scenes glimpsed during the celebration of the Eleusinian mysteries or traditional legends, for example "The Rape of Helen". He has a predilection for female bodies and paints them like a lover.

The activity of the decorators of large vases develops in parallel with that of the cup painters. There is the anonymous artist, working for the potter Kleophrades,* who can interpret, with great expressive force, human emotions on the face of Dionysiac figures. He also excels in the minute rendering of masculine bodies—ephebi, satyrs or heroes tired out after their athletic exercises. He applies himself methodically to the study of shadows and of three-quarter faces, an exercise his predecessors had shunned.

That sculpture was a pole of attraction for the painters of this period seems clear. Pure drawing, in which the calligraphic trace predominated, is now a thing of the past. The artist strives after mass by reconstructing the human body, treated in realistic fashion, in the centre of his vision. In this way the painter recovers the plasticity of the muscular masses as shown in movement, the torsion of the limbs and trunk. The effect is formal, reflecting the maturation in style made evident by comparison of the statuary of the period with the ephebi presented on the kylikes, amphorae and kraters.

These relationships become obvious when one examines the work of the "Berlin painter". Differing in temperament from the "Kleophrades painter", he succeeds to perfection in marrying the decoration of a vase to its shape. His preference is for isolated figures, silhouetted on the black ground which sets them off in all their plastic elegance.

Classical art

"The greatest of all marvels is man." This line from Sophocles sums up the fifth century ideal.

The Greeks have reached a great epoch in their history. Having repulsed the Barbarians, they take pride in their might. Serene in the face of calamities which destiny and the will of the gods have yet in store for them, they put their confidence in human worth in all its grandeur. They exalt it in statuary idealising the athlete's body, or in painting which pays respectful homage to the beauty of the ephebi, and also in the building of majestic sanctuaries to honour the city's protective deities, who have shown their justness in the triumph of the spirit over brute force. Art, both religious and civic and always of noble stamp, expresses general concepts, appeals to the spirit rather than the heart and hovers in the rarified domain of the Platonic idea.

Using political events as the yardstick, it is customary to make the classical

57

period coincide with the years following the Persian wars (470-446). This is the time when Athens is rebuilding her ruins and asserting her power. The apogee of these years is reached with the glorious principate of Pericles.* But then comes the Peloponnesian war against Sparta and her allies, culminating in the disaster of Aegospotami* and the city's subjection.

It seems preferable to replace this system of dating by another. Thus, the first phase of the classical period, lasting until about the middle of the century, bears the imprint of Polygnotos of Thasos, the most famous fresco painter mentioned in the literary sources. From 450 Pheidias is the dominant figure, which means that sculpture exerts a very marked influence over all the arts, so much so that one can speak of a "Pheidian period" even in painting. In the last years of the century, decadence is not far off, morals become relaxed, mannerism is all the rage and alongside the monumental movement appears that of the "florid style", so-called from the abundance of its decoration.

Signatures become rare. One of the last is that of Meidias,* towards the end of the century. It seems as though the painter-potters, overtaken by monumental painting, are resigning themselves to accepting their defeat and therefore unwilling to regard their work as anything more than simple craftsmen's products, unworthy of bearing their creator's name.

From the early years of the century, having surmounted his technical difficulties, the artist can resolve the multiple problems presented by the interpretation of what is

58

Attic cup (detail)
Young musician
6th century B.C.
Paris, Louvre

real. The "severe style" yields to what can be called the "free style". From now on the eye is shown in profile, an important characteristic which enables one to identify precisely the works belonging to this period.

The creator asserts his individuality and imposes his vision on a whole epoch. Down to the end of Greek art, one is thus in a position to follow the evolution of styles through the personalities of the artists.

The innovations distinctive of this period are due largely to the Athenian Mikon and to Polygnotos, his younger contemporary. Our information concerning Mikon as a person is scant indeed. It is known that his fame rivalled that of the painter from Thasos and that they collaborated in the decoration of several public monuments, which explains the confusion among many of the chroniclers over the attribution of their works.

Mikon is praised for his skill in portraying horses and scenes from the Amazon wars, replicas of which are to be found on several vases of this period, probably versions of his *Combat of the Greeks and Amazons* in the Stoa Poikile. His very famous *Battle of Marathon*, which he is said to have executed with Panainos, brother or nephew of Pheidias, must have been both majestic and moving. Equally admired were his *Departure of the Argonauts* and *Deliverance of Theseus by Herakles*. Bolder than Polygnotes in his choice of subjects, Mikon often adopts his techniques for the interpretation of space.

As for Polygnotos himself, it would be fruitless to try to trace his career,

Athenian horseman
About 500 B.C.
Paris, Louvre

since the ancient authorities confine themselves to a few observations, literary descriptions which are insufficient for a definition of his style. A native of Thasos, he came to Athens and was granted citizenship in reward for his decoration of the Stoa Poikile free of charge. In the course of a long career—he was still alive about 444—he was entrusted with numerous works referred to by Pausanias, the Elder Pliny and others, who certainly do not stint their praise. Mention is made in particular of his decorations to the temple of the Dioscuri at Athens, to the sanctuary of Theseus, the panels of the Stoa Poikile and other minor works at Plataea,* Thespiae and elsewhere. But his most celebrated works seem to have been the two compositions for the Lesche of the Cnidians at Delphi, *The Capture of Troy* and *The Underworld.* Pausanias describes them minutely, giving the poses of the characters, whose identity could be gleaned from inscriptions, some singularity of colouring or clothing, or the wealth of mythological and literary allusion. His signature was incorporated in a distich attributed to Simonides: "Polygnotos, native of Thasos,* son of Aglaophon, painted the *Fall of Troy*". These scraps of information may not permit us to pass aesthetic judgment, but they nevertheless clarify the problems the artist encountered and the solutions he found for them. The need to develop a subject in height instead of as in the past filling the surface with superimposing friezes, leads him to dispose his figures, without perspective, on different levels and on thin lines denoting the variation in the terrain. It thus came about that figures painted at the base of a fresco were placed at nearly half the height of those painted at the top. The notion of pictorial space had been suggested. The celebrated Orvieto* krater by "the Niobid painter" takes up this innovation. As with Polygnotos, the influence of the theatre is again evident, the "landscape" is suggested by an arbutus, a flower scattered discreetly here and there, like the "props" in contemporary drama. We have reached the period when the tragedies of Sophocles and Aeschylus* were enjoying such enormous success.

The painting of Polygnotos is significant as much for its content as for its technical innovations, and many ancient authors praise his incomparable gift for rendering the psychology of his characters: their feelings and passions were written on their faces. One thinks, surely with justification, of the "masks", comic or tragic, worn by the actors. Aristotle remarked that the figures of Polygnotos went beyond what is true and attained the "sublime". "Ethos", the heroic bearing of the spirit, is a quality on which Aristotle insists; in designating Polygnotos the most "ethical" of the painters Aristotle gives his approval to the moral standards to which his works bear witness and recommends them to young people as subjects for meditation, guides to the formation of character. The painting of Polygnotos, nourished on civic values, thus takes its place beside the inspiration of the dramatists as an expression of the ideal of the classical world in process of formation.

One might be cautious about the innovations ascribed to this artist were it not for the fact that a whole group of potters, who profited by his teaching, show the same prepossessions. On the other hand, the new iconographic repertory entails a modification to the shapes of vases, whose surfaces must be made to lend themselves to the display of much-peopled compositions and animated scenes. The cup is therefore ousted by the "volute" amphora and by kraters of various types: calyx, bell, column.

The large "Orvieto krater" by the "Niobid painter" is an eloquent commentary on the methods of Polygnotos and a confirmation of the Lesche of the Cnidians. On one side it shows the callous massacre of the Niobids by the gods. On the other we see warriors preparing for a campaign. Athena and her protege Herakles can be identified from their attributes. It has been suggested that the theme was an allusion either to the preparations preceding the battle of Marathon or else to the expedition of the Argonauts, painted by Mikon at this same period in the sanctuary of the Dioscuri.

The distribution of the composition over superimposed planes, the wavy lines indicating inequalities in the ground and partially concealing the bodies, recall not only the schemas of the painter from Thasos but also the method of projection used by Mikon.

The introduction into vase painting of an element of life and truth corresponding to the pathetic sentiment of the period declares itself for the first time with the "Penthesileia painter", who owes his name to a cup at Munich. Achilles is shown plunging his blade into the Amazon's bosom. According to tradition, at this supreme moment the queen requited his love; passion and despair are reflected in this dying look.

Furthermore, the dithyramb and satiric drama played some part, even greater than that of Aeschylean tragedy, in determining painters in their choice of subject.

About the third quarter of the fifth century Athens is at her height. The victory over the Persians reinforces her moral and political ascendancy and in particular the "idea of the city". Paying honour to the gods, protectors of the city, decorating their temples in magnificent style, are essentially patriotic actions. This was the climate Pericles could so subtly exploit to add embellishment to a city already rich and powerful. He strengthens the fleet, erects a third defensive wall, completes the dockyards at Piraeus and reduces the bounds of the empire. The transfer of the allies' treasury from Delos* to the Acropolis in 454 and control over its funds secures to the city the revenues necessary for the execution of major works. An army of artists, craftsmen and labourers is set to work under the orders of the architects Mnesikles* and Iktinos* and the sculptor Pheidias. The fame of Athens spreads throughout Greece and is carried abroad. Athens becomes the intellectual and artistic centre of Hellas. For twenty years the city is one vast building site, where one after another temples, porticoes, public monuments, adorned with a host of statues, bas-reliefs and frescoes, rise to completion. The most divergent theories and doctrines are propounded and freely debated in public. All religions and beliefs are respected. Criticism, even some measure of opposition, is received with tolerance.

Art could not fail to benefit from this liberal audience. If the second quarter

Cup by Douris
Eos and Memnon
Early 5th century B.C.
Paris, Louvre
▼

Amphora by the "Berlin painter"   ▶
Athena
First quarter of the 5th century B.C.
Bâle, Ciba collection, Dr. Käppeli

of the fifth century had seen the blossoming of monumental painting, from 450 it is sculpture, particularly the works executed for the Parthenon by Pheidias and his pupils, which will dominate the plastic expression of the period. Just as the temple friezes and metopes presented to the dazzled eyes of the faithful nothing less than a "narrative" of mythological and legendary events (panathenian processions, contests between gods and giants, Lapiths and Centaurs, the historic struggle of the Trojan war, prefiguring the wars with Persia, the birth of Athena), in the same way painting catches up with the preoccupations of sculpture, loses its character of a mere method of decoration and becomes "language". The monumental movement which predominates over all other tendencies during the course of the Pheidian period flows from elements clearly connected with the classical conception of sculpture. The subjects are inspired by themes from myth or epic. The scenes have a reticent and hieratic quality. The purity of the drawing allies itself with the simplicity and dignity of the poses. The people, extricated from archaic schemas, move with a restrained elegance which recalls the noble simplicity of the statues of the Parthenon. One also notices that attempts at rendering light and shade have been abandoned, as painter-potters

realise that graphic drawing adapts itself better to the character of their style.

Although of less importance than in the time of Kimon, the pottery of the Periclean age nevertheless includes the work of some original talents. The "Achilles painter", the first known to have specialised in white lekythoi, is one of the most famous. His earlier style still bears the stately imprint of the "Berlin painter", whose pupil he was. He owes his name to a red-figured amphora decorated on each side with a single figure, Achilles and Briseis. The majestic yet easy stance of the hero and the balance of the drapery recalls the prototypes of Polykleitos.*

Concurrently with this "noble stream we find subjects from daily life being treated on small vases, aryballoi, oenochoai, cups and pyxides. These pots, designed for a bourgeois clientele, attract a whole galaxy of painters who delight in capturing the air of refinement and daintiness surrounding women at their intimate moments: young girls at their toilet or bath, lovers' meeting, nupital ceremonies. Here beauty is no longer being sought after as plastic expression; what counts is the charm of the subject. The minuteness of the drawing reminds one of miniature work, hence the name "miniaturists" often applied to the authors.

Although minor, the works of the "Eretria painter" stand out from the rest. On a vase from Eretria* he depicts the bridal preparations of the young Alcestis, assisted by the Goddess of Love, Harmony, Persuasion and Youth. Allegory here makes its appearance, as in sculpture. On the other face, Alcestis is seen in her boudoir reclining on the nuptial bed, receiving her friends. Carefully worked out, more concerned with effect than economy in its drawing, this work for all its smallness bears comparison as a composition with the sculpture of the Parthenon.

The lengthy war with Sparta (431-404), the ruin it brought in its train, the death of Pericles—none of these affected the development of art in the way one might have feared. The consequences only start to make themselves felt in the very last years of the century. Much weaker after the Sicilian catastrophe, the empire finally collapses, carrying the democratic regime with it. These prolonged struggles brought more than economic ruin, a profound change in moral attitudes. The ideals for which men had fought were re-examined, values and beliefs were subjected to close scrutiny by writers, philosophers and historians. Civic life passed through moments of crisis which disrupted the bond between the citizens, making them lose confidence in their institutions and disturbing their loyalty. Certainty gave way to doubt and the "eternal values" yielded place to less rigid principles. Despite this disillusionment, Athens continued to be a major artistic and intellectual centre, but the spirit was changed. At this period one sees signs of the advent of a new world, which will have its heyday in the following century. The relaxation of morals and the new mode of life deflect artists from the noble idealism of the Periclean epoch towards realism, a realism of charm and refinement. Severity is replaced by a sparkling and exquisite grace. On the Acropolis buildings continue to rise, the Erechtheion and the temple of Athena Nike, but the successors of the great architects succomb to the attractions of the Ionic order. In

Stamnos by Hermonax (detail)
Philoctetes wounded
Second quarter of the 5th century B.C.
Paris, Louvre

sculpture the past is also discarded and Kallimachos,* in animated and supple forms, evokes the sensuality of the female body.

This evolution naturally has its repercussions on vase painting. The "free style" is followed by the "florid". Decoration becomes profuse. A frenzy for ornament sets in, for garlands and swirling draperies. Persons, female persons in particular, decked out in jewellery and rich embroideries, invade the imagery. They are shown engaged in all their most frivolous pursuits, in the Gynaiaion or at their toilet, with a precision of detail which seeks to exalt their sensual power. Love and Desire flutter everywhere, personified as small winged figures, accompanied by inscriptions. A pronounced taste for garish colour shows itself. The red-figured technique, formerly so restrained, is brightened up by touches of white or gold, highlighting the richness of fabrics and gems. Even the shapes are modified, and the vases most in favour are the pyxides and the graceful arbyballos-like lekythoi.

Aison* is one of the last painters whose name has been preserved. One of his best-known lekythoi, presenting Eros offering apples to Adonis, shows what was permissible in the flirtatious, free and easy climate of the day.

But it is perhaps the "Meidias painter" who conveys to us better than anyone the atmosphere of this decadent world. With an exquisite graphic line, he is at pains to reproduce the most minute details, either by moulding or by underlining anatomical features or draperies with frivolous details. His subjects, drawn largely from mythology, are suggested by the Platonic dialogues. Eros, Aphrodite or Adonis, the gods of pleasure and love, have replaced the heroid figures. They recall the Victories of the temple of Athena Nike, and equally the Theseus of Parrhasios, who, according to Plutarch, "seemed to be fed on roses".

One could cite still other names from this *fin de siècle*, but from now on they are only isolated figures, devoid of any originality in inspiration or technique; pottery

◀ Cup from the workshop of **Euphronios**
(detail) *Theseus and Amphitrite*
About 500 B.C.
Paris, Louvre

Hydria by Meidias (detail)
Amorous scene
End of 5th century B.C.
Florence, National Museum of **Antiquities**
▼

◀ ◀ Brygos cup (detail)
Sack of Troy
First quarter of 5th century **B.C.**
Paris, Louvre

has entered on its decline. And at the end of the fifth century the collapse of the Athenian empire brings about an almost complete standstill in production, which lasts for at least twenty years.

Side by side with the traditional red-figured and black-figured manner, potter-painters were also intermittently producing vases using the white-ground technique. Even in the seventh and sixth centuries, many craftsmen made use of a white background to set off the silhouette or drawing. But the method met with little success and it is only in the following century one finds it applied systematically to certain categories of vase, in particular cups, alabastra and lekythoi.

The cup, having its medallion as a surface, lent itself better than any other shape to the imitation of major painting, the exterior walls being reserved as a rule for red-figured decoration. Among the most famous are those of the "Sotades painter",*

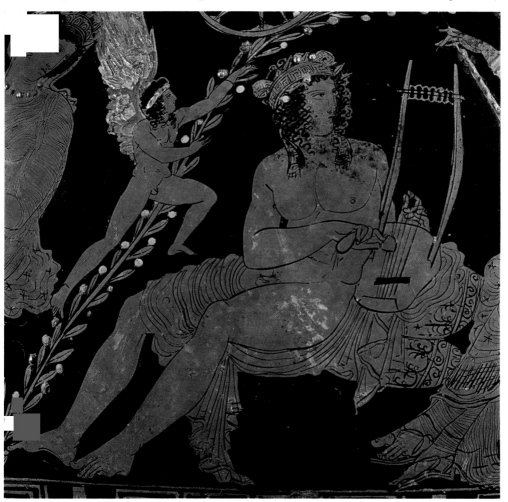

Stamnos by the "Berlin painter"
Infant Herakles and the snakes
First quarter of the 5th century B.C.
Paris, Louvre

which often give an inkling of space and a feeling for nature, rare in Greek painting of this period. The Kamiros cup of the "Pistoxenos painter" is also mentioned, remarkable for its delicate finish and harmonious use of colour.

During the Periclean period the lekythos shapes find most favour. They derive from black-figured vases of the sixth century and were used for libations. They might be placed either inside or outside the tomb. Those carrying funerary ornament provide valuable information concerning Athenian rites at this period. A fair number of these vases have retained all the freshness of their colours, whose range extended from red to blue and from green to yellow and black. The specialist in white-ground lekythoi is the "Achilles painter", who decorated quite a number of them and was an important influence on his contemporaries. Equally remarkable are certain pieces whose people recall those of Polygnotos.

In their drawing the vases of this period show a mastery and understanding never before attained. Figures in movement, presented three-quarters or full face, suggest, admittedly still in graphic fashion, but with precision and sharpness, a sense of volume and formal perspective.

It is towards the end of the century that the problem of perspective really presents itself.

Attic krater
Departure of an expedition
Second quarter of the 5th century B.C.
Paris, Louvre

Starting from conventions analogous to those of the ancient East (division of the surface into superimposed registers, seeing the effect as a whole, distribution of figures on different planes) the Greek craftsmen reach their goal once they have mastered axonometric foreshortening. The first advance is when the shields of warriors or chariot wheels are drawn as ellipses instead of circles. Next, the human figure is rendered three-quarters, while the quadrigae are given in profile. This is probably what Pliny means by "catagrapha" or "oblique images", whose invention he ascribes to Kimon of Kleonai.

In his "Treaty on Architecture" Vitruvius* mentions that Agatharcos of Samos, a painter contemporary with Zeuxis, was the first to paint "scenery" for an Aeschylean tragedy. On this occasion he wrote a book on the subject which seems to have attracted the attention of the philosophers Anaxagoros and Democritos and helped them to develop their theories regarding "natural perspective".

From what we know, it seems improbable that Agatharcos produced an organic solution to perspective in the sense of composing an entire "scene" round a single vanishing point. More likely he merely posed the problem, for which a logical solution would be found before the end of the Hellenistic age. Furthermore, the passage in Vitruvius does not state whether the "scenes" prepared for Agatharcos were painted

69

Attic alabastron with white ground
Barbarian warrior
First quarter of 5th century B.C.
Paris, Louvre

Krater (detail)
Centaurs in contact with the Lapiths
Third quarter of 5th century B.C.
Florence, National Museum of Antiquities

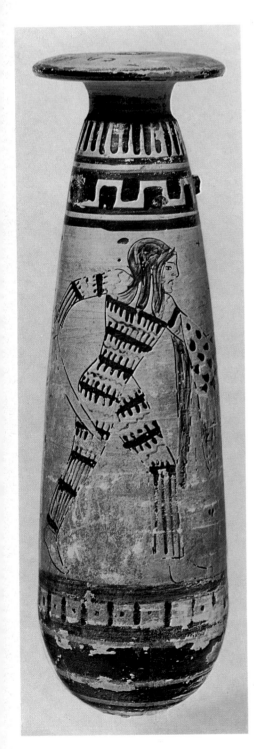

on cloth and hence by their nature susceptible to drawing in perspective; or whether he mounted his designs on wood and disposed the elements at different depths, which would have given the illusion of perspective.

If Polygnotos and Mikon applied themselves primarily to the problem of construction in space, Apollodoros of Athens,* known significantly as "Skiagraphos", painter of shadows, seems to have directed his efforts towards rendering mass by shadow effects. His "invention", as Plutarch terms it, seems to have consisted in rendering the mass of a body by the application of chiaroscuro and a progressive transition from light to shade. Apollodoros was a painter of great merit, famous throughout Greece as we learn from an epigram,* of Nikomachos. He was not a frescoist but an easel painter, working "al secio". Among his best known works mention may be made of a "*Priest at prayer*", probably a votive portrait, *Ajax struck by a thunderbolt*, admired later at Pergamon,* and *The Heraklides*. This last picture suggests the influence of Euripides.*

From now on, the artists achieve a high degree of perfection and this epoch can be considered the "Golden age" of painting. Public interest is growing, as we may conclude from the competitions which took place during the celebration of the Isthmian games or the Delphic festivals. The most famous painters are very rich men indeed; they are cosmopolitan travellers, men of culture and fêted by kings.

Two painters dominated the late century scene, Zeuxis and Parrhasios. The cheerful and racketty life they led—as exemplified by Alcibiades—can be imagined from the host of anecdotes still extant.

Towards 425 Zeuxis of Herakleia, still a young man, arrived in Athens, which for many years remained the scene of his activity. Towards the end of the century he was commissioned by king Archelaos of Macedon, patron of the arts, to decorate his palace at Pella;* Elianus reports that he was paid 400 minae (16 kg. of gold). Aristotle acknowledges the ideal beauty of his human figures, surpassing that of their models, while Lucian stresses the originality of the subjects treated by the master and his invention of new iconographic types.

Parrhasios of Ephesus does not appear to have reached the high level of perfection achieved by his rival. He started to work about 440 B.C. and is known to have been the author of the drawings for the shield of Pheidias' "Athena Promachos", of mythological works and, if Pliny is to be believed, of some small and scurrilous pictures, one of which belonged to the emperor Tiberius, who kept it in his bedroom. Like the vase painters, Parrhasios makes use of symbolic personification to portray human emotions: piety, clemency, pride, anger and humility. This study of psychology puts one in mind of the famous dialogue in which Socrates* and the artist discuss the possibility of interpreting human character in painting.

One passage in Pliny gives a fairly exact notion of Parrhasios' style: he made it his aim to render the volume and movement of bodies by suggesting the stereometric quality of the mass in depth, a problem which Skopas* would tackle in sculpture some decades later.

The fourth century

The beginning of the fourth century finds Greece at peace. Admittedly, the peace is only relative; if the period of violence is for the moment past, competing interests, social differences and jealousies portend the outbreak of fresh troubles. Profiting from the lull, Athens sets up a maritime confederation and founds a new empire, a dumping ground for her surplus and a market for her products. But hostilities start afresh and in thirty years enough damage will have been done to restoke the fires of jealousy and range the cities of the Peloponnese or Attica one against the other, thus preparing the way for the Macedonian conquest.

This disturbed period results inevitably in a profound moral upheaval, and although the civic spirit still carries weight, the traditional values have been shaken. Doubt and disbelief make inroads into men's minds, the old religious beliefs weaken and the sophists come into their own. Rationalism, the mean, classical sobriety give way to subjective thinking, the exaltation of the individual.

The backlash of these transformations will have a profound effect on the artists, and if there is little change in subject matter, the content is entirely different. Man is no longer an ideal being, an unassailable hero, invincible, ever-victorious over barbarians and monsters, but a circumscribed entity, whose actions will from now on be the object of psychological studies. It is no disgrace in the painter to descend from the Pheidian Olympus to the agora, for his choice to light on the ordinary mortal, reproducing his exact features, describing scenes from his domestic life. Art is to make the journey from idealism to realism. The striving for expression and pathos, the seductive charm of gracefulness and sensual appeal, such are the marks of the new ideal which the Hellenistic era will carry to its extreme limit.

The essence of these misgivings can be discovered from the efforts of the princi- painters. Three schools can be said to have flourished during this period, the school of Sikyon, the Attic or "Helladic" school and the Ionian or "Asiatic" school. With the exception of the first, these are not schools in the modern sense of possessing defined characteristics which would enable one to be distinguished from another. It is necessary therefore to speak in terms of the artists who formed part of them, rather than of the schools themselves. From the many highly flattering references to him, it seems that Apelles,* born at Colophon* and resident at Ephesus, must have achieved enormous fame. Pliny tells us that he "had a charm of manner, which earned him the favour of Alexander the Great". Apelles painted many portraits of Alexander, Philip and personages of their court, but his most famous painting is still the Aphrodite Anadyomene, contemporary with Praxiteles' statue. A great traveller, he turns up at Pergamon where he is said to have decorated a public building. But he concentrated chiefly on painting on wood. He employed only four wax colours and worked with brush and sponge to obtain chiaroscuro effects; he had invented a special glaze whose secret he always refused to reveal. He was praised for the precision of his drawing and

Attic Cup
Combat
5th Century B.C.
Florence, National Museum of Antiquities

the grace which distinguished his people. These elements are insufficient for us to form a judgment on his style and the books he wrote about his own painting have unfortunately vanished.

Protogenes,* a native of Xanthos in Lycia, was a contemporary of Apelles. He lived chiefly at Rhodes, where he decorated the great temple consecrated to Dionysus. It is reported that when Demetrios was besieging the city he refused to have it burned in order to spare a picture depicting the Rhodian hero Ialysos, on which the artists have been working for eleven years.

Portraiture and large compositions were not the only genres in favour with the public. Many realist "small masters" were painting genre scenes and still lifes. The vogue they enjoyed during the Alexandrine period seems to have been due to Piraikos, a native of Piraeus. Pliny says that he liked to paint "barbers" and shoemakers' shops, donkeys, cooking ingredients and other such things", which earned him the soubriquet "rhyparographos", painter of humdrum objects. "Rhyparography" and "rhopography"—the word is used by Diodoros in the sense of "still life"—are the two types of painting the ancient authorities contrast with "megalography", not because of the size of the canvas but by reason of the subject matter (scenes from bourgeois or peasant life, small landscapes).

The verism of this period, which shows itself above all in the use of chiaroscuro, is also brought out in a text of Pausanias referring to Pausias, who painted a glass cup in which the countenance of Drunkenness himself was seen as a transparency. The fame of this painter is due primarily to his skill in the use of encaustic,* a process particularly favoured by the school of Sikyon, where he was a pupil. The inventor of this technique is unknown and Pliny remarks: "Some people claim it was invented by Aristides* of Thebes and perfected by Praxiteles". In any case it had long been in current use both for architecture and for painting on stone. It was certainly known to Polygnotos and employed by Nikias on a large scale.

If the fourth century was the *grande siècle* of painting, the same cannot be said for pottery, which from now on plays an increasingly secondary role. The defection of the public was accompanied by the almost total closure of the Italian market, as local workshops became established there. The new schools, Lucanian, Apulian, Tarentine, Campanian will impose their own style and often also their own original shapes.

The vases in the "Gnathian style",* a technique practised especially at Tarentum, are of particular interest. What happens here is that polychrome figures on a black glaze replace the red figures, and give a much better idea of the progress accomplished in major painting.

Deprived of their Italian outlets, the potters of Kerameikos attempt to consolidate their old markets or look for new ones, in Cyrenaica and, above all, in the Cimmerian Bosporos.

The works of this period are of very unequal merit and, some happy exceptions

Attic white-ground lekythos (detail) ▶ Attic white-ground lekythos (detail) ▶ ▶
Dead man before his stela   *Dead man before his stela*
Last quarter of 5th century B.C.   Last quarter of 5th century B.C.
Athens, National Museum   Athens, National Museum

apart, show clear signs of retrogression. Industrialised, relegated to the hands of humble artisans reluctant to add their signatures, pottery will henceforth merely vegetate in the shadow of great art.

In this first third of the century there is decadence everywhere: compositions sag and are overloaded, the drawing is defective and scamped, there is frequent retouching in white, insipid pink or shrieking greens and reds, and much flashy gilding. The clientele is more interested in the subject than in the quality and finish of the workmanship, so the repertory is enlarged, to become one of the most varied in the whole history of Attic pottery. Religious themes abound and certain gods grow in importance and become humanised. Eros obtrudes himself, Dionysos is triumphant, Aphrodite becomes the goddess of spring, her epiphany is celebrated. The heroic spirit fades, Achilles falls into oblivion; when it comes to the Trojan exploit, men concentrate on the minor cycles, more in keeping with the amatory interests of the time. There are pictures of rapes, of clandestine meetings or ill-fated lovers, attributable to the influence of Euripidean drama. Woman from now on has a premier role. Her love life, her daily occupations in the gynaeceum are among the most frequent subjects.

Towards 370 a new style appears, to reach its height some twenty years later and in the Alexandrine epoch holding the field. This style, known as Kerch, which brings red-figured pottery to a close, is interesting for a number of reasons. The favourite shape appears to be the pelike, but the bell krater remains equally in favour, as also the oenochoe, the small-size lekythos and the lekane, a bowl with a lid intended to hold objects for the feminine toilet. The decoration is amatory in inspiration: for example the crouching Venus later taken over and popularised by sculpture. One notes also a recovery of interest in Eleusinian iconography, stimulated by the prevailing mysticism, and also in a theme of somewhat restricted appeal, the struggle of the Arimaspes with the gryphons, which flattered the Bosphoran clientele.

The Hellenistic period

The unification of Greece under the kings of Macedon and the conquests of Alexander give birth to a new form of civilisation, resulting from the fusion of the Oriental heritage with Hellenic tradition. The great centres of art and culture will now be Alexandria,* Antioch,* Pergamon and Rhodes. The death of Alexander and the partition of his huge kingdom seems to encourage a diversity in modes of artistic expression, although the common characteristics still remain. It is again the Ionian core which re-emerges, with its taste for the picturesque and for movement, its love of nature and of life.

But the Hellenistic ideal of this period is summed up first and foremost in its

concrete vision of reality. The triumph of verism and illusionism in art corresponds to the Aristotelian conception in philosophy and to the experimental and positivist outlook of the mathematical sciences, astronomy, medicine, and history. The artist scrutinises the human body with an attentive eye, describes its anatomical features and does not hesitate to point out physiological blemishes. The sense of pathos is heightened: physical pain contorts the body, moral suffering the countenance, the pangs of love exasperate the senses. A certain romaticism enters in, veiling the softness of the female figures in sadness and melancholy. This is also the day of the portrait, which gains in precision from its minute description not only of the features but also of the psychological expression of the subject.

This multiplication of poles of interest and thirst for originality inevitably brought weaknesses in their train. The picturesque is overdone, the more gossipy type of narrative makes a composition banal. The movement is distracting, breaking the equilibrium and the rhythm. The declamatory exaggeration of gesture and expression leads to a kind of mannerism.

Such is the complex appearance presented by the Hellenistic era, an amalgam of astonishing richness which by reason of its universal character will survive through Rome and Byzantium to keep its place in many domains of our Western culture.

It has been said that the Hellenistic age was the most brilliant period in the history of major painting. All the same, our knowledge of it would be very incomplete were it not for the existence of certain mosaics and funerary stelae which disclose something of its technical secrets and iconographic repertoire. The Roman frescoes,

Mosaic of *The battle of Alexander* (detail)
End of 5th century B.C.
Naples, National Museum

often inspired by or copied from Greek and Hellenistic originals, are a particularly valuable source of information.

Mosaic, already known to the Hellenes, shows an exceptional rise in the course of the last three centuries. It was, in fact, just as suitable as mural painting for the decoration of huge architectural ensembles, public buildings, princely dwellings or the villas of the wealthy.

One of the most famous is *The battle of Alexander* discovered at Issos. A glorification of the great conqueror and his victory over the Persians, this becomes one of the favourite themes in the Alexandrine cycle. The Ancients ascribe it to various authors—Aristeides of Thebes, Helenos of Alexandria*—but it seems more likely to have been the work of Philoxenos of Eretria,* a disciple of Nikomachos. This mosaic, which is of exceptional quality, appears to be a faithful copy of its original, judging from the self-imposed limitation to the four colours beloved by Polygnotos and the methods used to convey the idea of space (echeloning of the spears, disposal of the people on different planes, bold foreshortening, tonal graduation).

There are also the pebble mosaics of Pella, which add valuable information about the technical processes of the period. They are among the most representative and in them one finds a large use of shading and of shadows treated in blue, as in our modern painting. The mosaics of Delos mark an important stage in the evolution: small stone cubes have replaced the cobbles, thus opening up infinite possibilities of grading and shading.

The literary sources furnish very little on the subject of mural painting, which seems to have been reserved for royal residences. The only works to have come down to us are the funerary paintings on limestone or marble from various sites such as Alexandria, Cyprus and above all Pagasae,* where about a hundred have been discovered.

The advance in major painting makes pottery seem all the poorer by comparison. The tendency to imitate metal vases becomes more marked, to the point where the potteries lose almost all their interest in forms. However, the pictorial tradition is continued in the decoration. The motifs raised with a brush on a white ground express a certain feeling for nature, a tendency we find again on Attic vases. In this last phase of pottery, relief vases with a black glaze occupy a special place. The evolution of this technique resulted from a striving after novelty. On certain vases the decoration in polychrome relief, confined to the principal figures, is combined with pictures made by painting. On others, the entire decoration is treated in relief and picked out with gilding. The motifs are various, inspired by the Trojan epic or scenes from Euripidean drama. Some bowls with a matt finish are still being decorated with plant and geometrical motifs. The workshops of Delos were among the principal producers of vessels of this type which were manufactured in moulds, the decoration being printed with a puncheon. Other centres of production have been discovered in Russia, at Pergamos, at Athens and in Boeotia.

Tarquinia, necropolis
"Tomb of Fishing and Hunting"
About 520-510 B.C.

Etruscan Painting

The Etruscan spirit

Unlike our situation as regards Greek art, we know very little about the "phenomenon" of Etruscan art. In fact what we have here is a unique group of monumental paintings which spreads over the centuries from the seventh to the first B.C. demanding our admiration for its lofty style, and at the same time providing us with a fairly complete picture of the major art of the classical world, its aesthetic and its techniques. Concrete and anecdotal, this art is also a priceless document concerning the history, beliefs, customs and way of life of the Etruscan people.

Furthermore, for many centuries the Etruscans suffered an undeserved neglect. The reasons for this are remote and complex. They go back to the Greek and Roman authors who scarcely mention the Etruscans, because they found them disturbing. Happily things have now changed, and from the middle of this present century an ever-increasing interest has been shown in this civilisation so unjustly ignored.

There can be no understanding of Etruscan art and culture without a reference to religion. Etruscan religion was very different from the beliefs of the Greeks or Romans and came closer to those of the East; its doctrine, written down in sacred books, was compounded from traditional wisdom and a very strict ritual which governed private and public life. This complex of rules, doctrines and practices is often referred to by classical authors under the name "disciplina etrusca". A kind of divination, the "discipline" was based essentially on the relationship between the macrocosm and the microcosm. A terrestrial event was the manifestation of a divine event.

Among the Etruscans divination took various forms. The practice of haruspicy or examination of the liver, the seat of life, was very widespread, as also the interpretation of thunder and lightning and of all prodigies which "explained" natural phenomena.

A fatalist spirit, which deprived the individual of all freedom, dominated each daily action. It was impossible to omit the ritual without incurring divine punishment.

The base of the discipline rested on a well-defined cosmogony and theology. However, systematic study of the Etruscan pantheon remains an arduous undertaking, because it was invaded at a very early date by elements from Greek religion and mythology.

The world of the gods was made up of Tinia, lord of the thunder and corresponding to Zeus, Uni (Juno) and Minerva (Athena). This apparently was the triad introduced at Rome, where the Capitoline temple, built in the time of the Tarquins, Etruscan kings, was raised in its honour.

The beliefs about which we know most, thanks to the discovery of necropoleis, are those which dealt with the after life. The spirit of the dead man lives on in the tomb and requires clothing, food, utensils and furniture.

81

Tarquinia, necropolis
"Tomb of the Bulls"
Charging bull and erotic scene
Second half of 4th century B.C.

From the sixth century B.C. this primitive conception of survival after death is replaced by a belief, Greek in origin, in the Kingdom of Shades, Hades, which is inhabited by demons. Pessimism and the fear of death set their seal on the paintings. Eita (Hades), Persipnai (Persephone), male and female demons and Charun (Charon) make their appearance and the joyful scenes of the past yield to bloodshed and massacres.

Because of its singularity and variety, Etruscan art is one of the most significant in all antiquity.

It has been labelled "peripheral" and "regional", because having fallen under the influence first of the East and later of Greek universalism, Etruscan art always tended to waver between imitation of the models in question and the manifestation of an expression proper to itself. However, despite this lack of tradition, the native genius, rejecting sterile mimesis, was strong enough to avoid the total sacrifice of its individual spirit and aspirations to the exotic accretions. It is this very conflict, and this absence of a uniform trend, which gives Etruscan art an originality whose contours can be defined though their clarity should not be exaggerated.

Conditioned by the physical structure of the country, by the craft materials available in the soil, the plastic arts show diversity and the poles of attraction alter with the region or city and from one period to another. Thus in the main urban settlements one finds specialised schools flourishing, maintaining continuity in production and in spirit, jealously perpetuating themselves from generation to generation: stone-cutting (Chiusi), the secrets of metal-working (Vulci), the love of painting (Tarquinii), the technique of figured terracotta (Veii), skill in vase-making (Caere) and in ceramic work (Arezzo).

From the early days of their history, this sea-faring people, open-minded and

Tarquinia, necropolis
"Tomb of the Augurs"
Scene of the wrestlers
530 B.C.

susceptible, are found establishing fertile contacts with the East and with the Greek world. The products they import stir the imagination of their creative artists; and if these are willing to learn from the experience of others, they do so to recreate it all the better in spontaneous and original forms.

The religious rules binding on the artist curb his speculations and experiments, prevent him from having that universal vision of the world one is aware of with the Greeks.

The Etruscan has a deep feeling for nature, shown in his familiarity and sympathy with the forces of the Cosmos,* with animals and plants, whose multiple facets he takes pleasure in describing, with freshness and realism, on vases, cinerary urns or the walls of tombs. His love of life is made concrete in the tranquil assurance of his description and narration. His forms, lyrical, exuberant, almost baroque, blossom into scenes full of movement: the hunt, the delights of fishing, frenetic dances, athletic sports. Unlike the rationalist Greeks, the Etruscans, naive and spontaneous, are drawn towards polychromy, to garish colours, to complex shapes loaded with decorative elements.

The Eturian artist knows nothing of Greek idealisation. He aims deliberately at realistic and concrete effects. With a wealth of characteristic detail, funerary painting show aspects of the life of the deceased, and gives us genuine portraits of the dead.

83

Funerary painting

Etruscan funerary painting, together with the much later Roman, is the source which brings us into direct contact with ancient art. Spanning some seven centuries, from the seventh to the first B.C., it offers an enormous spread of motifs and information. It also makes possible a mental reconstruction of the monumental Greek painting with which it was contemporary.

The most significant portion of Etruscan painting is composed of mural decoration to the tombs hewn from the living rock of the necropoleis found in the neighbourhood of settlements. Despite their abundance, however, they represent only an infinitesimal portion of what once existed but has now been destroyed, whether by subsidence, humidity, erosion or, indeed, by men.

For the visitor these cities of the dead are an arresting sight, with their streets, tenanted by silence and mystery, along whose length narrow doorways give access to an uninterrupted succession of conical tumuli or to monumental corridors hollowed out from the tufa and running down deep into the ground. In the volcanic zone of Viterbo there is a different arrangement. Tombs sculpted from the rock itself reproduce, with great simplicity of line, the architectural facades of houses and temples in the oriental style. At Orvieto, on the other hand, the shape resembles that of rectangular city dwellings, with doors and windows giving onto the street.

The experience becomes still more impressive when one penetrates to the interior of the tombs. Whatever the form, the houses of the dead are a reminder of their dwellings in the world of the living. As a rule, one is greeted by a central hall, flanked by secondary chambers. It is quite common to find along the length of the walls stone benches on which the sarcophagi rested, with false doors or windows simulating wood. Every effort has gone into the ornamentation, to leave the dead man for eternity with the memory of his life on earth, and at the same time make his lengthy sojourn pleasureable. Reliefs sculpted actually in the tufa itself are rare. A few, representing animals and objects in common use, have been found in the "tomb of Reliefs" at Cerveteri. It is more usual to find long painted friezes, occupying the upper portion of the walls.

During the primitive period, the use of painted decoration is known throughout Etruria. Later, a few exceptions apart, it is confined to Tarquinii, where we shall be able to follow its most significant phases.

The frescoes of the funerary hypogea* in themselves offer an enormous field for investigation. But our documentation is again complemented by vase-paintings, sarcophagi and terracotta plaques.

Apart from the "Villanovan", strictly local, production which is in evidence from the eight century, Etruscan pottery falls far short of the high degree of perfection achieved by the Greek pottery already invading the Italian markets. The superiority of the Greek puts the Etruscan industry at a disadvantage right from the start, inter-

fering with its development and restricting it to monotonous imitation.

Essentially a maritime region, dependent on trade for its prosperity, Etruria came under the influence of the chief Mediterranean centres. Thus, instead of developing the spiritual resources welling up from within, she allowed herself to fall under the spell exerted by the culture of more evolved regions. That is why, if one excepts an initial period of local experimentation in the eight century and a second, orientalising phase in the seventh and sixth, the chronology of Etruscan art in the following centuries runs parallel with that of Greek art.

In the eighth century B.C. Etruria was elaborating a homogenous culture, quite distinct and much more evolved than that of neighbouring regions, and which is known as "Villanovan".

Next, thanks to the exploitation of the iron ores of the island of Elba, within a very few years settlements start to multiply from the Tiber* to the Arno. Trading becomes intensive all along the Tyrrhenian coast and even threatens that of the Phoenicians* and the Greeks. Etruscan ships ply the Mediterranean, carrying the precious metal eagerly sought after by eastern merchants and receiving in exchange luxury products, stuffs, carpets, painted vases, jewels. The native artists, dazzled by such richness of motifs, refined techniques, and boldness in conception, set themselves to learn from the East. The geometrical Villanovan motifs give way to fantastic animals, sphinxes, gryphons, chimeras, winged lions affrontant, framed by stylised elements drawn from the vegetable kingdom.

The first witnesses to painting date from the end of the seventh and the beginning of the sixth centuries and are divided between central and southern Etruria. Faded rough outlines in the tombs at Cerveteri and Veii, and sketches made by nineteenth century travellers who saw paintings which have now disappeared, show us animals or decorative details of Syrian, Cypriot or Aegean derivation.

The field of pottery is much richer, and here the most ancient works to come down to us date from the end of the eight century. These are the vases known as "impasto", with abstract stylised shapes, a double inverted cone or a simulation of

86

Tarquinia, Museum
"Tomb of the Olympiads"
Painting on cloth

Tarquinia, necropolis
"Tomb of the Triclinium"
Female dancer
About 470 B.C.

Tarquinia, necropolis
"Tomb of the Augurs"
Scene of the wrestlers
530 B.C.

complicated anthropomorphic or animal forms. The carefully executed ornamentation is composed of geometric motifs: dots, lines, circles, chevrons, swastikas. There are already indications of a very advanced taste in decoration, which will develop still further among the artists of the following generations.

The tombs have yielded a particular type of pottery called "bucchero", produced by local workshops. The lustrous black colouring was obtained by a special process of fumigation during the firing. This technique, perfected at a very early date, made it possible to create vases with very thin walls which could compete with their metal prototypes of eastern origin. These extremely audacious and often original shapes are covered with exuberant compositions. Geometric decoration is replaced by an oriental repertory of stylised figures displayed in parallel zones and in relief. The production of vases continues throughout the sixth century, but the shapes become clumsier and overloaded.

The golden age

The sixth century sees Etruria in its heyday, both on sea and on land. Her traders and adventurers succumb to the luxurious life of their Eastern and Greek rivals, and since they now favour the Ionian style it is adopted likewise in Etruria.

The principal centre of the style was Caere, whose close relations with the Greek world are confirmed by the presence of a Caeretan treasury at Delos. Caere must have been host to numerous artists—potters, sculptors or painters—from all over the Greek world; their work vied so keenly with the products of their homelands that it is often difficult to distinguish the one from the other.

The most ancient witnesses to painting we possess are terracotta plaques from Caere. They belong to an intermediate period towards the middle of the sixth century. The surface was covered with a transparent polished slip on which the subject was first traced and afterwards coloured. The method of execution was probably that ascribed to Kraton of Sikyon. Placed side by side, they formed a frieze to cover the walls of tombs or public buildings. They survive in considerable numbers, the oldest being the Boccanera plaques, named after their discoverer. Certain details suggest Corinthian influence, although there are others more reminiscent of Ionia or the East.

If we are endebted to Caera for our knowledge of painting's remoter past, we must go to Tarquinia to discover the most imposing and complete ensemble of funerary decoration.

The artists who worked on these tombs were inspired by the world of Greek mythology; guided, however, by their innate realism, they replace the gods and heroes by people captured in the actuality of their everyday life, dressed in the local style, and so break with the archaic schematisation of their Hellenic models.

Tarquinia, necropolis
"Tomb of the Leopard"
Man playing the double flute
Beginning of second quarter of 5th **century**

A visit to some of these tombs is an initiation into a fairy world. The oldest, called the Tomb of the Bulls (c. 540 B.C.), offers a felicitous illustration of a Greek myth, that of Achilles preparing to kill Troilus, son of Priam. The composition is Ionic-Aegean in inspiration, but the presence of trees and plants testifies to the specifically Etruscan love of nature. Furthermore, the naive treatment of the animals and the liveliness of the colouring reveal an artist who shares the tastes of his time and country.

The frescoes of the other tombs present the life of the period in its most varied aspects and liveliest manifestations.

Those in the Tomb of the Augurs show funeral games taking place in the presence of two bearded personages. A bloodthirsty duel is in progress, similar to the contests of Roman gladiators. The harshness and realism which looms out at us from these scenes affords some insight into the curious world of Etruscan beliefs. The people's expression, their heaviness, the primitive, almost brutal air, are elements foreign to the Graeco-oriental models and bring these paintings close to the hydria of Caere.

The huge landscape of the Tomb of Fishing and Hunting leads us into an entirely different domain. Here the people are but one element in the naturalistic decoration. This vision of space in which many-coloured birds wheel in full flight, the accuracy of pose in the young men fishing or diving, reveal an unexpected talent for this period. One must go back several centuries, to the swallows of Phylakopi, to discover a comparable feeling of elegance and spontaneity.

To set against the exceptional freedom of execution and the verve displayed in this painting we have the serenity and moderation of the frieze in the Tomb of the Baron, the acme of pictorial art at Tarquinia in its archaic phase. Everything suggests that these domestic scenes—the proffering of a cup to a noble and dead lady and a three-cornered conversation—are to be interpreted as a funerary rite. But its great plastic value attaches above all to the incomparable harmony of the composition, regulated rhythmically by intervals, negotiating the wide gaps between the people by means of plant motifs. These last, stylised and elegant, are silhouetted on the clear ground and are early testimony to the ideal of refinement specific to recent Ionian trends, whose reflections can be seen on the sarcophagi of Clazomenai or the red-figured Attic vases of Epiktetos.

Unlike the Greeks, the Etruscans are almost invariably indifferent potters; they content themselves with the imitation of imported models. However, the "Caeretan", hydriai and "Pontic" amphorae deserve our attention. Greek emigrants must certainly have worked on the decoration of these vases, in collaboration with local craftsmen. They transpose the Ionian motifs and adapt them to the taste of their clientele, particularly susceptible to polychromy and liveliness of colour.

The political decline of Etruria and the economic crisis which ensues steadily deprive her of her former pre-eminence in the Mediterranean markets; in her isolation, she remains unaffected by the major changes introduced by Polygnotos. At the end of the fifth century no "classicism" arrives to supersede the archaic phase, which will continue for some time yet.

Classicism proper will make itself felt only in the course of the fourth century, when it has already become the heritage of the Greek world.

At the beginning of the fifth century other influences appear, noticeable in the obvious connections one finds between Etruscan painting and that of exponents of the "severe style", for example the "Kleophrades painter". The changed conception of the after-life at this period works towards pessimism. The motifs become cruel: the artists' imagination is haunted by a Hades inhabited by figures of horror, bloodthirsty and vengeful demonic creations crop up even in mythological subjects whose provenance is Greek.

The happy alliance of Attic pottery with a certain Etruscan penchant for the unreal, already manifest in the Tomb of the Baron, recurs in the decoration to the Tomb of the Triclinium (c. 470 B.C.). The painter has been able to develop in lyrical fashion the motifs exploited earlier—the banquet, the dancing—by adding some human emotion, which is in contrast with the harsh realism of the preceding period. In style and spirit this painting bears a close affinity to the Tomb of the Funeral Couch which dates from before 460 B.C.

In addition to these major works we have those of lesser importance, executed by artists who were able to profit from the example of potters working in the "severe style". But from now on the subjects are reduced to a merely ornamental academism or adapted to a provincial taste, not wholly devoid of a popular flavour. This is so with the paintings at Chiusi (Tomb of the Monkey, c. 480-470 B.C.), where an atmosphere of village junketing replaces the noble style of Greek athletic competitions.

Towards the middle of the fourth century the artists of Etruria were apparently again in contact with Greek classical art, as is attested by an exceptional document, the "Amazon" sarcophagus discovered at Tarquinia, a rare example of a casket with painted decoration. The subjects have been taken from famous compositions of Amazon battles.

The author was probably a Greek of southern Italy. The finesse of the drawing, the projected shadows and light and shade effects, the foreshortenings and feeling for space, the moving expression on the Amazon faces, make this a remarkable work, especially in this period of decadence.

Towards the end of the fourth century funerary painting revives at Tarquinia and Orvieto in a new form. In it the artists give utterance to the grief weighing on their people as a result of their political decline and the consequent threat of extinction.

The group in the Tomb of Orcus, comprising two burials of different periods linked by a passage, is the most characteristic example of the change. The older of the two, almost completely destroyed, showed Velia feasting with her husband. A fragment depicting the head of this noble lady is the sole portrait to have come down to us

from ancient art. Hellenic influence is evident in the purity of the drawing and the stylisation of the features. Equally remarkable is the expression on this face. It suggests the terror of the young woman in the presence of Charon, winged and grimacing, brandishing his hammer. The later part of the tomb dates from the end of the third century and presents an adaptation of the theme of the Greek after-life. The painting in the passage relates in minute and cruel detail the blinding of Polyphemos by Ulysses.

The vase painting of this period offers nothing original. The Etruscan potters are content to reproduce, sometimes in felicitous fashion, the fine red-figured Attic vases of the severe style and later on of the florid style. The fourth century will see workshops established at Vulci, Chiusi and Falerii, to compete with Hellenic production. A few of the cups are well turned-out, for example the Aurora amphora, the best work to come from the workshops at Falerii.

External influences

It is in the Hellenistic era that the fate of Etruria is sealed. The terrifying spectre conjured up by the loss of one city after another, the growing power of Rome—everything contributes to the atmosphere of increasing heaviness and doom.

The art of the period is by no means insensitive to the situation. Hellenistic art, born out of the great Alexandrine adventure, chimes perfectly with the secret yearnings

94

"Amazons" sarcophagus
Greek attacked by two Amazons
4th century B.C.
Florence, Archaeological Museum

Tarquinia, Etruscan necropolis
"Tomb of Ovcus"
Profile of an Etruscan Lady
End of 4th century B.C.

of the Etruscans, and the sombre auguries of their imminent disappearance only accentuate their anguish in the face of death, expressed in nightmare images or in scenes now of blood-drenched violence, now of hectic rejoicings. The fate of man in the next world, which is the dominant preoccupation in spiritual life, becomes a major theme. And the spirit of realism will lead eventually to verism in portraiture, especially noticeable in sculpture, but also to be found in some surviving examples of painting.

These two tendencies manifest themselves in funerary painting. The Tomb of the Shields, as we know from numerous inscriptions, belonged to a rich aristocratic family who did not neglect to gratify their pride by bequeathing their titles and portraits to posterity. The decorations revolve round the traditional funeral feast.

The artist reproduces the features of his subject with an exceptional mastery of expression. This is not merely a matter of their external appearance; he achieves a more intimate veracity, of the phschological order. Although of unequal value and somewhat haphazard in execution, the group in this tomb represents a significant moment in the Etruscan art of portraiture.

A different climate prevails in the François Tomb at Vulci (second or early first century). Savage themes of the underworld, furnished by Greek mythology, are mingled with descriptions of historical events of local significance. Among the many compositions featuring portraits of tomb proprietors, that of Vel Satie is considered to be the only portrait in the whole of Antiquity to have been executed true to life.

Elsewhere one sees mythological scenes mingled with traditional Etruscan motifs; *The massacre of the Trojans by Achilles* has an extraordinary realism and ferocity, further underlined by the presence of Charon and of demons.

Winged giants, recalling those of the sculpted frieze at Pergamos, are to be found on the pilasters of the Tomb of the Typhon (first century B.C.). In this monument, the last in the Etruscan funerary series, the influence of the Hellenistic art of Asia Minor, already preponderant in sculpture, is very much in evidence. On the wall of the sepulchre a scene, unfortunately very badly damaged, shows a procession of people marching into the next world, spurred on by a horde of demons flourishing hammers, torches and musical instruments. These facial expressions, wholly imprinted by grief and horror at the prospect of death, achieve a degree of intensity rarely equalled. The pictorial ensemble of this tomb, in certain technical and formal characteristics, already presages the Roman art which will be its successor.

The pottery of this period continues to imitate, with no great originality, the Hellenistic prototypes. However, an important change takes place in the course of the third century. The traditional red-figured technique is replaced by the fabrication of vases with a black coating on which the motifs in varied colours are painted. This new process is employed in southern Italy and spreads at least into the central regions. The iconographic repertoire continues to draw on mythological or historical subjects together with domestic scenes or themes of the after-life. But the end is at hand, to plunge the culture of the Etruscans and their art in undeserved oblivion.

Evidence and Documents

Intimate Greece

The Greeks introduced into their house the world of the air and the plants. The cadaver of Pompeii, a city of Magna Græcia, built and decorated by Greeks, is covered with flowers. In the inner rooms, in the markets, everywhere are garlands of flowers, fruits, and leaves; there are birds and fishes, dense, shining, fiery still-life pieces surrounding false windows and painted floors which open on perspectives of streets and squares, of architecture and streets. It is doubtless only a translated, Latinised Greece, different from classic Greece and much affected by influences of Alexandria, of Asia, and inspired above all by the sea-sky, the vegetation, the red rocks, the flame, and the wine mulled on hot coals. Theocritus was a Syracusan, it is true. But on the soil of Greece there are bas-reliefs, vase-sculptures. Tanagra groups—satyrs, nymphs, young women, dancers, divinities of the woods and torrents around whom we hear the purling of water, the rustle of leaves, the lowing and sharp bleating of the beasts, and flutes laughing and crying in the wind. And if surrounding nature stilled her voices for a moment to let Pheidias commune with himself as he wrote into the human form alone his understanding of the world. Sophocles went to sit in the grove of Colonna, the grove of orange trees with its many crickets where the brooks ripple under the moss; Pindar, the rugged poet of the north, while journeying to the games by routes which took him to gorges and beaches, picked up on his way some formidable images, full of the sky and the ocean; Eschylus, from the top of the Acropolis of Argos, watched the night sparkle, and from the most distant past of Hellas a cool breeze was blown. Egean art is already alive with forms of the sea. The sea wind, the water of the river, and the murmur of the foliage are witnesses to the meeting of Ulysses and Nausicaa, whom the hero compares to the stem of a palm tree. Does not Vitruvius affirm that the Doric comes from the male torso, the Ionic from the female torso?

In any case, this rather limited Pompeiian art, made up, as it is, of recollections and distant imitations, and due almost entirely to the brush of hired decorators and of house painters, breathes the animal and the material world, the swarming and confused world that surrounds us. How young it still is, despite the old age of the pagan civilisations; how vigorous it is with all its vague mossiness; how profound and full of the antique soul! What persuasion there is in its power, and, on the monochrome backgrounds—red, black, green, or blue—how broad and spontaneous the stroke is, how sure, how intense in expression, and how living the form! Amors, dancers, winged geniuses, gods or goddesses, animals, forms nude, draped, or aureoled with wavy gauzes, legends, battles, and all the ancient symbolism so near the soil live again here, with a slightly gross sensualism and with the candor of the workmen who interpret, certainly, but with that calm, that almost unspoiled freshness, that virginity of life which were known only to the ancient world. The dancing forms appear half veiled, with their pure arms and pure legs continuing the pure torso, like balanced branches. The nude bodies emerge gently from the shadow, floating in their firm equilibrium. Here and there are implacable portraits with large, ardent eyes—with life in its brutal austerity, undiminished by any visible intermediary. At times, side by side with the Greek soul, and bearing a germ of academism that, fortunately, is still unconscious, there is that ardent expressiveness which, thirteen centuries later, was to characterise the awakening of Italy. It is to be seen in that "Theseus Victorious over the Minotaur", which the great Masaccio would have loved. It is an anxious, uneven world, with currents of influence running through it in every direction, but fiery and brilliant, rotten at the top, and yet ingenuous underneath.

See in these portraits the sense of immensity that is in the gaze, how the great figures are steeped in thought, and how a tremor seems to run inward through their living immobility. This arrested life is almost terrible to look upon. One would say that it had been suddenly fixed, as if seized by the volcano at the same hour as the city was. Impressionism, do you say? Yes, in its fire, in its breadth, in the way in which the movement is instantaneously surprised; but however much weakened, however enervated the voice of the artisans of a corrupt and sceptical age, this painting expresses a power of comprehension and a depth of love that only a few isolated men attain to-day. It is the only real renascence of Greek heroism. It responds, like the "Hercules of the Belvedere" and the Venuses of the valley of the Rhone, to the shock of Hellenic intelligence as it meets with Latin force and, in a flash, creates an art complete in its vigor, its ardent life, and its feverish concentration.

Although these paintings are not, properly speaking, copies (if we admit that a copy is possible and that the copyist, whether mediocre or touched with genius, does not in every case substitute his nature for that of the master), although they are only reminiscences, the transplantation of Greek works on a renewed soil, it is through them that we can get an idea—even if a distant one—of the painting of antiquity, which the crumbling of the temples has wiped out. The most celebrated frescoes of the dead city recalled the works of Polygnotos, Zeuxis, Parrhasios, and Apelles. The painting related the ancient myths and the story of the national wars. At first it knew flat colours only, very much simplified, doubtless, very brilliant and hard tones, brutal in their oppositions, before modeling appeared with Parrhasios. The lines which enclosed the powerful polychromy must have had the firmness of the uninterrupted curve which the passage of the hills to the plains and of bays to the sea taught to the men who were at this time making the gods. Always decorative in its beginnings, it undergoes the fate of the painting of modern schools, where the easel picture appears when the statues descend from their heights on the temples to invade the public squares, apartments, and gardens. Like sculpture, this painting had to bend to the will of the rich man. But doubtless it retained its character better, being more supple, more a thing of shades, more individualistic, more the master of saying only what it did not want to hide. I see it, after Parrhasios, as somewhat like Venetian painting around Giorgione and Titian: ripe, warm, autumnal, with an evanescent modeling in the colourful shadows and dazzling in the parts which stand out and which seem turned to gold by the sap from within. It is less fluid and musical, however more massive, more compact. Oil painting has not been discovered, and the wax renders the work slower and less immaterial.

In any case it has preserved until our time, through Pompeii, the perfume of the Greek soul, of which it hands on to us one of the most mysterious aspects, far better than does the art of ceramics, which has traced that soul for us in hardly anything more than its external evolution—in such matters as composition, superficial technique, and subjects. The role of ceramics is limited, with the little terra cottas, to representing the national industrial art of Greece—which is already saying a good deal. But it cannot pretend to stand for more than the reflection in the popular soul of the flowers gathered by certain minds throughout the nation.

Hundreds of workshops had been opened practically everywhere, in Athens, in Sicily, in Etruria, in Cyrenaica, in the Islands, in the Euxine, in a place as distant, even, as the Crimea. The most celebrated painters of cups, Euphronios, Brygos, and Douris, worked with their workmen, often repeated themselves, copied one another and rivaled one another in activity so as to attract patrons. Through the goodly communion of their work, through their continual exchange and emulation, they founded a powerful industry.

Industrial art, however, in spite of these powerful roots, is so limited by its very purposes, that it cannot pretend to such high intention as that of the art which governs the sculpture of the gods. On the other hand, it avoids, for a much longer time, the double snare of pretentiousness and of fashion. Thus it dies less quickly and renews itself more readily. Diderol was right in re-establishing the dignity of the industrial arts. He was wrong in placing them on the same level with the others. The sculptor, and more especially the painter, in his struggle with the material, is guided only by the quality of the material. The purpose of the object allows it to move in so wide an area that the liberty of these artists knows no other limits than those of the infinite space in which occur the relationships of intelligence and sensibility with the whole universe of sensations and images. The artisan is confined between narrower frontiers by the function of the furniture or the ornament on which he works, and also by its size. A fresco and a thimble do not offer identical means to their creators. If the murmur of the soul can be as pure, as touching, in one as in the other, the elements of the symphony are far less numerous in the latter case, and infinitely less complex.

In addition, the workman must arrange, in such a way, the ornaments with which he wants to decorate the object, so that they will follow the contour of its forms, to modify themselves according to its volume and its surfaces, and, like himself, accept a role which excludes all others and which is, even so, of an inferior order. And thus it is that only in very rare cases do we discover on the sides of even the most beautiful Athenian vases a hint of that logical composition which places the great sculpture on the plane of the universal. Forms elongate and become parallel to wed the flanks of the amphoras, to make them straight and to give them spring. They stretch in encircling rings around the cups, the vases, and the bowls as if to drag the pot along in a spinning movement. Here and there, undoubtedly very often, in an ensemble at once fiery and sober, easily read at a glance, black on red or red on black, there are admirable details, drawing as pure as the line of the landscape, incisive as the mind of the race, and suggesting the absent modeling by its direction alone and its manner of indicating attitude and movement. For the workman as for the sculptor of the temple, the mould of the Archaic is broken, nature is no longer a world of immutable and separate forms, but a moving world, constantly combining and disuniting itself, renewing its aspects and changing the elements of its relationships at every second.

The form of these vases is so pure that one would say it had been born unaided, that it had not come from the hands of the potters, but from the obscure and permanent play of the forces of nature. We have a vague sensation before these vases, as if the artist were obeying the hints of the wheel as he presses in or swells out the clay, thickens the paste or spreads it. When the wheel hums, when the material whirls and flies, an inner music murmurs to the moving form the mysterious fluctuation which gives songs and dances their rhythm. Grain, breasts, round haunches, closed flowers, open flowers, twining roots, spherical forms of nature—the central mystery of them all sleeps in the still hollow of the vases. The law of universal attraction does not control the suns alone, but all matter moves and turns in the same circle. Man tries to escape from the rhythm, and rhythm always draws him back again. The vase has the form of fruits, of the mother's belly, and of the plants. The sphere is the matrix and the tomb of forms. Everything comes out of it. Everything returns to it.

Save in the case of the great Panathenaic amphoras which have the severity of design proper to their use, the Greek vase almost always welcomes you with a charming sense of the intimate. When it recounts the adventures of war or interprets the old myths, it humanises itself delightfully. Very often there are children at their games, men in their workshop, women at their toilet, long, undulating, and rich forms indicated with a continuous line. The familiar painting of the Egyptian husbandman told of the work of the fields. The familiar painting of the Greeks, a people of traders and talkers, speaks rather of household work.

Elie Faure

History of Art   Volume I

Texts concerning painting

At length art emerges from its chaos: it discovers light and shade and through this difference the contrasting colours heighten each other's effect. Later lustre is added, a value different from light. What lies between lustre and shadow is called "bright-dark"; the place where the two colours meet and shade into one another is called "demi-tinted". (Pliny.)

Knowing how to paint the bodies and setting of objects is without doubt a great merit, but many painters have thereby acquired glory; drawing the outlines of a body, enclosing a painting within a precise contour, it is this which is rarely done with success. For the limb should turn and finish in a manner which gives the impression that there is something else behind it and even of seeing what it hides. (Pliny.)

Here is an odd thing worth remembering: we appreciate the last works of artists and the pictures they leave unfinished more than their completed works . . . This is because in them we still see traces of the drawing and catch the thought of the artist unawares. (Pliny.)

Line drawing was invented by Philokles the Egyptian or by Kleanthes of Corinth; the first to practise it were Aridikes of Corinth and Telephanes of Sikyon; these artists, still without using any colour, were already shading with lines the interior of their outlines. Ekphantos of Corinth was the first to colour his drawings, it is said by using fragments of broken pots. (Pliny.)

. . . the inventions (of Eumaros) were perfected by Kimon of Kleonai. It was he who invented "catagrapha" or profiles, and represented the figures in different positions, looking backward, upward or downward; he marked the attachments of limbs, made veins stand·out and also discovered the art of folding and wrinkling drapery. (Pliny.)

If one paints in a confused way, even with the most beautiful colours, it will not give as much pleasure as a picture painted simply in white. (Aristotle.)

We should imitate good portrait painters who, when they will their own features even though they are not aiming at an exact likeness, paint themselves best. (Aristotle.)

The best copyist will bear away the crown only if he makes it his aim to imitate that which is most beautiful. (Aristotle.)

(The creator) starts by drawing all the outlines, then he chooses the colours and the flesh-tints and the harsh tones as if the demiurge were in truth a painter of nature; this, in fact, is how painters, once they have sketched their design, give colour to the beings they wish to represent. (Aristotle.)

Here is a way to give colours their value: it consists in making them shine through their relation to one another, as painters sometimes do, placing another tint over one more vivid. (Aristotle.)

Stranger: In the art of imitation, I distinguish first that of copying. Now to copy is to reproduce the proportions of the model in length, width and depth; further, it is also to add to each part of the drawing the colours appropriate to each, in a way which produces a perfect imitation.
Theaetetus: Well then! Do not all who imitate try to do the same thing?
Stranger: No, at least, not those who paint or sculpt on the large scale. You know very well that if they gave the beautiful figures they represent their true proportions, the upper parts would appear to us too small, the lower too large, because we see the former from a distance and the latter close at hand. Therefore our modern artists, not bothering about truth, measure the porportions of their figures not by reality but by appearance.
Theaetetus: You are right, that is what they do. Now, this first kind of imitation, is it not right, since it resembles the object, to call it a copy?—Yes—And this part of the art of imitation, should it not be called, as you have already told us, the art of copying? —It should be so called.
Stranger: But then, what names shall we give to that which seems to resemble the beautiful, because the perspective has been managed with beauty in view, but which, when one has liberty to consider it at leisure, no longer resembles the object whose image it is? Since it really seems to resemble, is it not a phantom? (In effect. Is it not then a considerable part of painting and, in general, of the art of imitation? Indisputably. And the art which produces a phantom instead of a faithful copy, should not this be called very precisely phantasmagoric? Indubitably.) Here then we have two species of the art of making simulacra of which I was speaking, the art of copying and phantasmagoria.

It is as though someone, finding us painting human figures, reproached us for not placing the most beautiful colours in the most beautiful places of the figure; reproached us that the eyes, although the most beautiful, were being coloured not red but black. It seems we could justify ourselves quite well by saying: but, my friend, it is not our business to paint eyes so beautiful that they no long appear to be eyes, and so with the other parts; look then and see whether, by giving to each its appropriate colour, we have not produced a beautiful whole. (Plato, *Theaetetus*.)

(Apollonios) says to Damis: "Do you believe there is an art of painting?" "Yes, if there is a truth." "And what does this art do?" "It mixes colours together, blue with green, white with black, red with yellow." "And why do painters make this mixture? Is it only to give their pictures lustre, as women do when they paint themselves?" "It is to better imitate, better reproduce for example a dog, a horse, a man, a ship and everything illuminated by the Sun. Painting even goes so far as to represent the Sun, sometimes mounted on four horses, as he is said to appear here, sometimes setting the sky ablaze with his rays and colouring the ether and the dwelling of the gods." "Painting, then, is the art of imitating?" "It is nothing else. If it were not this, it would merely be an absurd jumble of colours thrown together by chance." "The things we see in the sky when the clouds part to form centaurs, chimeras and even, by Zeus, wolves and horses, are not these works of imitation?" "Apparently." "Is God then a painter, Damis? Does he leave the winged chariot on which he rides as he orders all things human and divine, to amuse himself by painting trifles, like children on the sand?" Damis blushes as he realises the absurd consequence to which his proposition has led. However Apollonios shows no contempt as he takes it up again, for there was nothing bitter about the discussion. "Do you not rather wish to say, Damis, that the clouds move across the sky at random, representing nothing, or at least no image intended by God, and that it is we, accustomed as we are to imitation, who imagine and create these images?" "That is better, Apollonios: it is much more likely and more in keeping with reason." "There are then two imitations, Damis, one which consists in representing objects both with the mind and with the hand, that is painting; the other by which the mind alone represents them?" "There are not two," says Damis, "there is but one, which is complete and called painting; this is the one which can represent objects with the mind and with the hand simultaneously. The other is but a part of this: it is the process by which, without being a painter, you conceive and imagine figures; but you would be incapable of tracing them with the hand." "Is this because you are one-handed or maimed?" "Not at all, it is because you have never touched pencil, brush or colours and have not studied painting." "Then, Damis, we are agreed on this point that the talent for imitation comes from nature and painting from art. What we have said could likewise apply to sculpture. Painting itself does not, as I think you are saying, always consist of a melange of colours; for one colour alone sufficed for the ancient painters; it was only later that four, and afterwards a greater number, came into use. Furthermore, is not a drawing in which the shade and light is marked, even without the use of colours, still a painting? In such drawings one sees, in effect, resemblance, figure, character, modesty or boldness: however colour is lacking there, the tint is not represented, nor the lustre of the hair or beard; the bronzed and the white find themselves represented by one and the same tint. For example, we use only white to paint this Indian, but for all that he will appear black; the snub nose, the frizzy hair, the bulging cheeks and a certain expression in the eyes, all this darkens the features one sees as white and to every eye at all experienced represents an Indian. I would also freely admit that a person who looks at a painting should himself also possess the faculty of imitation. You would not, in effect, know how to appraise a painting representing a horse or a bull if you cannot represent to yourself the animal so depicted. Not to love painting is to despise reality itself, it is to despise the kind of merit which we find among the poets, for painting, like poetry, delights to offer us the features and actions of heroes; it is also to have no respect for the science of proportions, which links art with the very use of reason. If one wanted to speak whimsically, one could say that painting is an invention of the gods, thinking, that is, of the different aspects of the earth, whose fields are painted as it were by the Seasons, and of everything we see in the sky. But to trace art back seriously to its origins, imitation is one of the oldest inventions, as old as nature herself. We owe its discovery to some clever men, who called it sometimes painting, sometimes plastic art. Plastic art itself is divided among several genres: for to imitate with bronze, to polish the Lygdos or the Paros, to work in ivory, all this comes into plastic, as too, by Zeus, does the art of engraving on metals. Painting consists of the use of colours, but not only of this, or rather from this unique medium painting derives greater benefit than another art with numerous resources. In effect, painting represents shadows, varies the expression of looks, and thus shows us anger, grief or joy. Plastic has no means of giving eyes their proper lustre; in the representations of painting they may be brilliant, bluish green, black. Hair is light fawn, fiery, golden. Everything has its colour, drapery, weapons, houses and apartments, woods, mountains, streams and the air which envelops all things. Many artists have excelled in this art; many cities, many kings have been passionately in love with it. (Philostratos of Lemnos.)

It was with four colours only, for the whites that of Melos, for the yellows the sil of Attica, for the reds the sinopis of Pontus, for the blacks atramentum, that Apelles, Aetion, Melanthios and Nikomachos executed their immortal works, illustrious painters, one of whose pictures would sell for the price of all the treasures of a city. (Pliny.)

Colours are sombre or vivid. They are so either by their nature or by mixing. The vivid colours, supplied to the painter by his employer, are minium, armenium, cinnabar, chrysocolla, indigo, purple. The other colours are sombre. To whichever category they belong, some are natural, others artificial: sinopis, rubrica, paraetonium, melinium, eretria and orpiment are natural colours; the others are artificial, those we already mentioned in connection with metals and among the common colours, ochre, burnt ceruse, sandarac, sandyx, syricum, atramentum. (Pliny.)

In ancient times there were two methods of encaustic painting: on wax, and on ivory with the cestrum or small graver. It continued so until people started painting warships; for this a third method was added to the preceding; it consists of laying on the melted wax with a brush, a kind of painting which, applied to ships, is affected neither by the sun nor by the salt water nor by the winds. (Pliny.)

(Painting with minium) cannot withstand the action of the sun and moon. To preserve it, once the wall is properly dry, one must apply with a hair brush a layer of very white

Punic wax melted with oil and then burn it again until it sweats, by the application of glowing gall-nuts; after this one must smoothe it by rubbing first with tallow and then with really clean linen cloths, as one does to make marble shine. (Pliny).

Those who paint by placing "purpurissum" with egg over a layer of sandyx obtain the lustre of vermillion; if they want to make purple, they place "purpurissum" with egg on a layer of blue. (Pliny.)

The earth of Chios, dissolved in milk, is used for rewhitening walls. (Pliny.)

Gum is made with sarcocolla, which is the name of both the tree and the product; it is most useful to painters and physicians, resembling the powder of incense; also the white is preferable to the red. (Pliny.)

The best glue is made with the ears and genital organs of bulls . . . but also nothing is easier to fake, with old skins, boiled down shoes even. The Rhodian brand is the most reliable and is therefore used by painters and physicians. (Pliny.)

The preparation of every kind of black is completed in the sun: black for writing, with an admixture of gum; black for coating, with an admixture of glue. Black which has been dissolved in vinegar is difficult to wash off. (Pliny.)

Wax darkens if one adds paper ash, since, by mixing with the anchusa (small plant with a red juice) it reddens and, thanks to the colours, can take on the most varied tones to render the most diverse aspects and serve innumerable uses: notably the protection of walls and weapons. (Pliny.)

Is it possible, on seeing a huge mansion, magnificent, everywhere lit up, glistening with gold and flowering as it were with paintings, not to want to describe it? When an educated man contemplates beautiful objects he is not content to enjoy them only with his eyes; he does not remain the dumb spectator of these beauties; he tries his best to become possessed by them and express them by some word of gratitude . . . But here you see the difficulty: to reconstruct such pictures without colours, without figures, away from the place itself: for it is a poor thing to paint only in words. (Lucian.)

When the walls have been coated with three layers of sand and as many of marble, they should display neither cracks nor any other defect. But when their endurance has been tested by subjecting them to a prolonged battering with "baculi" (a type of beater) and polishing has given them the glossy white of marble, then, since colour is applied at the same time as the polishing, the walls can shine with a most brilliant sheen. As for the colours, when they have been laid carefully on a still wet plaster, they never come away but are fixed for ever; this is because the lime, having lost its moisture in the kilns and become attenuated and porous, absorbs everything with which it happens to come in contact, as though in need of food; and through mixing, if gathers the seeds or principles of the other elements, and thanks to them solidifies in all its parts. Hence when it dries it is reconstituted to the point of appearing to possess the qualities proper to its nature.

Thus plastered surfaces which have been well prepared do not become rough and when they are cleaned their colours do not flake off, unless, that is, they have been carelessly applied and on a surface already dry.

So, when the surfaces for painting have been prepared in the way just described, they will be able to retain their firmness, sheen and vigour into a ripe old age. (Vitruvius.)

When, in decoration, vermillion is applied to the wall finish of enclosed apartments, it preserves its colour without alteration. But in open places—that is to say, in peristyles or exedrae or other places of this sort where the sun or moon can penetrate with their brilliances or rays—then the place painted in vermillion is affected, the colour changes, and losing its proper virtue turns to black. (Vitruvius.)

Preparing whortleberries in the same way and mixing them with milk, the "tectores" make an elegant purple. (Vitruvius.)

The soot is collected and in part compounded with gum to make writing ink; the rest, mixed with glue, is used by house-painters for the walls. If these substances are not to hand, one must meet the situation in such a way that no delay results. Vine-shoots or pine needles must be burnt; when they have been charred the fire must be put out; then they must be pounded with glue in a mortar. In this way one will obtain a black for painter decorators which is not without elegance. (Vitruvius.)

The Ancients who first made mural decorations started by imitating the veining and flagstone arrangements of marble; then various combinations of animals and triangles in sil.

Later, they came to imitate the very forms of buildings, the jutting out ledges of columns and gabbs; to design for open places such as exedrae, because of the width of the walls, scenes like the frontispieces to dramas in the tragic, comic or satyrical style; to decorate promenades, because of their length, with a variety of landscapes, making their pictures suitable to the special features of the setting. (Vitruvius.)

Texts concerning the painters

Polygnotos

This illustrious artist (Polygnotos) painted a building at Delphi, and at Athens the portico called Poikile, which he did for nothing, whereas his collaborator Mikon made sure that he was paid for his share in the painting. (Pliny.)

Polygnotos of Thasos was the first to paint women with transparent drapery and to give them head-dresses of different colours. He was also the first to introduce into painting those great improvements which consist in opening the mouth, showing the teeth, replacing the old rigidity of the face by a variety of expressions. (Pliny.)

Above the Kassotis is a building containing pictures by Polygnotos. This is an offering from the Cnidians. The Delphians call it the Lesche, because in the old days they would meet there to discuss serious matters or pass the time in bantering and telling stories. . . . Then as you enter the building, all the pictures on the right represent the capture of Ilion by the Greeks and the departure of their fleet; the other half of the picture, on the left, shows Ulysses in Hades . . . (Pausanias.)

It is not right for young men to contemplate the pictures of Pauson but rather those of Polygnotos or any other painter or sculptor who has given expression to morality. (Aristotle.)

Appollodoros

Appollodoros, the painter who first invented colour-mixing and the graduation of shades, was an Athenian. His works bear this device: "It will be easier to criticise than to imitate me". (Plutarch.)

Zeuxis

The famous Zeuxis, who was a master of his art, ignored or very rarely treated subjects which have been popularised and become too well known, heroes, gods, or battles; ceaseless in his pursuit of novelty, when he conceived some unusual or startling design he deployed on it all the resources of his art. Amongst other *tours de force*, Zeuxis once painted a female Centaur flanked by her sucklings. (Lucian.)

Parrhasios

Parrhasios painted the *Demos of Athens* in a very ingenious personification. He showed it, in effect, as fickle, choleric, unjust, volatile and at the same time easily moved, merciful, compassionate, glorious, lofty, humble, bold and faint-hearted, in a word everything at once. (Pliny.)

Pamphilos

Pamphilos was of Macedonian origin. But he was the first painter to have studied all the sciences, above all arithmetic and geometry, without which, he declared, no one could attain perfection in art. He never gave lessons for less than one talent or the rate of 500 denarii per year. This was the fee paid to him by Apelles and Melanthios. (Pliny.)

It is said that Pamphilos, Apelles' teacher, not only painted in encaustic but what is more taught this technique to Pausias of Sikyon, the first to become famous in this genre. (Pliny.)

Apelles
Apelles had a charm of manner which earned him the favour of Alexander the Great. This prince often came to visit him in his studio, for as we have already said, he decreed that no other painter should paint his portrait. (Pliny.)

His inventions have been of benefit to all other artists. But there is one thing no one has been able to imitate. When his pictures were finished, he gave them a coating so light that while giving the picture, because of the reflection of the light, a very clear colouring, and protecting it from dust and dirt, the coating was visible only when the picture was within hand's reach. The coating had the further great advantage that it prevented the too vivid impact of the colours from wounding the sight, as though the spectator was looking through a specular stone. By some undiscoverable means, from far away this process gave a darker tone to over-brilliant colours. (Pliny.)

(Apelles) says that all Protogenos' qualities were equal or even superior to his own, but that he scored on one point: he knew when to withold his hand from a picture. By this memorable lesson he intended to say that working with excessive minuteness is often damaging. (Pliny.)

The texts cited here are taken from the Recueil Milliet, "Textes grecs et latins relatifs a l'Histoire de la Peinture ancienne", edited with translation and commentary (under the patronage of the Association des études grecques) by Adolphe Reinach, former member of the Ecole d'Athènes, Vol. I, foreword by S. Reinach. Librarie C. Klincsieck, 1921.

Pericles the Olympian

It is not proposed to describe the history or evolution of Greek temple-architecture but simply, in connection with this sketch of Pericles' personality, to make a few marginal observations on that "love of beauty in simplicity" which is manifest in the great monument to Athena and her people.

When the Persians departed in 479 B.C., the Acropolis was no more than a vast cemetery of heaped up stones and broken statues. Themistocles and Cimon applied themselves to what was most urgent—military necessity: they rebuilt the two walls which rise from the rocky hill, the former building on the north side, the latter on the south. These walls which completely encircled and protected the hill-top were constructed so as to extend the summit-plateau of the Acropolis and allow of its surface being more or less levelled. In the space between the upper edge of the wall and the plateau, the authorities carefully buried the statues of the maidens painted in red and blue which the preceding generation had set up in the days of its prosperity. These statues have only been excavated in our own days; their colouring was still fresh.

Now Pericles saw in art a means of asserting the pre-eminence of Athens over the whole Hellenic world. The Parthenon was to dominate Greece as it has, in its calculated perfection, dominated land and sea and reigned through the centuries.

Pericles kept an eye on everything. He discussed the architect's plans as well as the choice of materials; supervised the execution, visited the work-yards and controlled the expenditure. In the year 450 Pheidias was appointed general overseer of the work on the Acropolis. This Athenian sculptor, who was now forty-two years of age, was already known for several pieces of work executed in different parts of Greece. It was in the same year, 450, that he erected the statue of Athena on the Acropolis. With her curls confined by a plain ribbon, her aegis held loose and the helmet in her hand, she appeared as the embodiment of youthful splendour. The spear had been transferred to her left hand, serving now not as a weapon but as a support for the arm. This was not the Warrior Maid but the bright image of Peace restored. In later years Pheidias erected two other Athenas on the Acropolis, one of them a colossal and warlike figure that bespoke the artist's mastery of bronze. It also bespoke Athenian imperialism, suggesting that peace was an unstable thing, hardly restored before war once again loomed on the horizon. Lastly there was the Athena Parthenos, idol and guardian of the city and the city's treasures, shining in gold and ivory amid the gloom of her sanctuary. One can imagine this tall and ornate ivory statue, clad in gold and framed at the end of the double colonnade of the cella. Her tranquil countenance, which seemed to come alive in the deep shadows, towered above piles of precious offerings, rich fabrics spread over marble tables, and shield suspended from the columns. She was the proud and splendid image of Athenian supremacy.

In addition to all this, Pheidias carved with his own hands a large part of the decorations of the Parthenon. He carved or at any rate inspired the continuous

Ionic frieze, in which his chisel created the procession celebrating the Festival of Athena with a simplicity so near to the ideal that one's heart almost stops beating as one gazes at it. Here we see the cavalcade of young horsemen, the slow march of the elders whom age has scarcely touched, the metics and the subject-peoples with their offerings, and the maidens who, clad in their long dresses as in the very adornment of modesty, have for this rare occasion emerged from the gynaeceum. There is no expression on these faces, not even a smile; it is as though, on approaching the gods who await them at the end of the frieze, men acquire the gods' impassivity. But this was the first time that plain citizens, and not gods or heroes, were represented on the frieze of a temple. Both Pericles and Pheidias had so desired it.

Pheidias also personally carved the sculpture in the two pediments which are too much damaged for one to describe them; we can only say that here divine power is expressed not in the violence of some bold gesture but in the nonchalance of godlike muscles in repose. Caught motionless, as it were, in the midst of some act, the strength of the gods would appear limited; yet in this calm repose their strength, though unexercised, seems indeed limitless and divine.

Pheidias let his pupils carve the greater part of the metopes in the Doric frieze.

This artist lived in the closest intellectual sympathy with Pericles, and the latter remained faithful to him when Pheidias was in disgrace, in 432 B.C., and even until he died in prison shortly after his condemnation.

For eighteen years he had been director-general of the works on the Acropolis. Nothing had escaped his severe yet always constructive criticism. He had taken as much interest in the general planning of the various monuments as in the smallest technical detail of their construction. No doubt the architecture of the Parthenon owes him a good deal more than its sculptural decoration.

Pheidias may doubtless be reckoned with Sophocles and Pericles as one of the three men of genius produced by this historic era. They collaborated in the Parthenon, a monument created by collective effort. We may recall in this connection that, at the very moment when he was composing the *Antigone*, Sophocles was chairman of the financial commission—the College of Hellenotamiae—which administered the public treasure levied from the allies. These three men were engaged, if not in the same political direction, at least in the service of an enterprise by which, through the building of the new Acropolis as through the flowering of Sophoclean drama, the greatness of the people governed by Pericles found splendid expression. Sophocles, for his part, did not think that the *Antigone* and the *Oedipus* dispensed him from the duty of presiding over an important commission with the intelligence and loyalty of a good citizen.

The beauty of the Parthenon is of the simple kind; but this simplicity, like the simplicity of all great works of art, is the outcome of something rare and complex, something that escapes our first impression.

At first glance, indeed, the Parthenon looks like a purely geometrical construction: the solution of a problem in geometry in which the material is assembled in perpendiculars, circles, straight lines and triangles in such a way as to stand up in successful equilibrium. It seems to have been built of dimensions. This was because it represented the culmination of generations of study on the part of Greek temple-architects who had been seeking out the right proportions between the length and breadth and the height of the building; the ratio between the diameter and the height of the column, the ratio between the breadth of the column and the space between the columns, the ratio between the diameter of the column at its base and the diameter at the top of the shaft—and many others.

Yet this quest of mathematical perfection would, if it could be fully accomplished, only satisfy our reason. It would please us in the manner of a theorem correctly solved. But the Parthenon does not please us in this way, or rather not merely in this It satisfies and prolongs our organic sensation, our joy in the consciousness of life. It touches us as if it were, not an Absolute, but a living thing. It is an order, but an order as mobile as that of natural orders and species.

Andre Bonnard

"History of Art", vol. 1
"Greek civilisation: From the Iliad
  to the Parthenon"

The painted tombs of Tarquinia

We arranged for the guide to take us to the painted tombs, which are the real fame of Tarquinia. After lunch we set out, climbing to the top of the town, and passing through the south-west gate, on the level hill-crest. Looking back, the wall of the town, mediaeval, with a bit of more ancient black wall lower down, stands blank. Just outside the gate are one or two forlorn new houses, then ahead, the long, running tableland of the hill, with the white highway dipping and going on to Viterbo, inland.

"All this hill in front," said the guide, "is tombs! All tombs! The city of the dead."

So! Then this hill is the necropolis hill! The Etruscans never buried their dead within the city walls. And the modern cemetery and the first Etruscan tombs lie almost close up to the present city gate. Therefore, if the ancient city of Tarquinia lay on this hill, it can have occupied no more space, hardly, than the present little town of a few thousand people. Which seems impossible. Far more probably, the city itself lay on that opposite hill there, which lies splendid and unsullied, running parallel to us.

We walk across the wild bit of hilltop, where the stones crop out, and the first rock-rose flutters, and the asphodels stick up. This is the necropolis. Once it had many a tumulus, and streets of tombs. Now there is no sign of any tombs: no tumulus, nothing but the rough bare hill-crest, with stones and short grass and flowers, the sea gleaming away to the right, under the sun, and the soft land inland glowing very green and pure.

But we see a little bit of wall, built perhaps to cover a water-trough. Our guide goes straight towards it. He is a fat, good-natured young man, who doesn't look as if he would be interested in tombs. We are mistaken, however. He knows a good deal, and has a quick, sensitive interest, absolutely unobtrusive, and turns out to be as pleasant a companion for such a visit as one could wish to have.

The bit of wall we see is a little hood of masonry with an iron gate, covering a little flight of steps leading down into the ground. One comes upon it all at once, in the rough nothingness of the hillside. The guide kneels down to light his acetylene lamp, and his old terrier lies down resignedly in the sun, in the breeze which rushes persistently from the south-west, over these long, exposed hilltops.

The lamp begins to shine and smell, then to shine without smelling: the guide opens the iron gate, and we descend the steep steps down into the tomb. It seems a dark little hole underground: a dark little hole, after the sun of the upper world! But the guide's lamp begins to flare up, and we find ourselves in a little chamber in the rock, just a small, bare little cell of a room that some anchorite might have lived in. It is so small and bare and familiar, quite unlike the rather splendid spacious tombs at Cerveteri.

But the lamp flares bright, we get used to the change of light, and see the paintings on the little walls. It is the Tomb of Hunting and Fishing, so called from the pictures on the walls, and it is supposed to date from the sixth century B.C. It is very badly damaged, pieces of the wall have fallen away, damp has eaten into the colours, nothing seems to be left. Yet in the dimness we perceive flights of birds flying through the haze, with the draught of life still in their wings. And as we take heart and look closer we see the little room is frescoed all round with hazy sky and sea, with birds flying and fishes leaping, and little men hunting, fishing, rowing in boats. The lower part of the wall is all a blue-green of sea with a silhouette surface that ripples all round the room. From the sea rises a tall rock, off which a naked man, shadowy but still distinct, is beautifully and cleanly diving into the sea, while a companion climbs up the rock after him, and on the water a boat waits with rested oars in it, three men watching the diver, the middle man standing up naked, holding out his arms. Meanwhile a great dolphin leaps behind the boat, a flight of birds soars upwards to pass the rock, in the clean air. Above all, from the bands of colour that border the wall at the top hang the regular loops of garlands, garlands of flowers and leaves and buds and berries, garlands which belong to maidens and to women, and which represent the flowery circle of the female life and sex. The top border of the wall is formed of horizontal stripes or ribands of colour that go all round the room, red and black and

113

dull gold and blue and primrose, and these are the colours that occur invariably. Men are nearly always painted a darkish red, which is the colour of many Italians when they go naked in the sun, as the Etruscans went. Women are coloured paler, because women did not go naked in the sun.

At the end of the room, where there is a recess in the wall, is painted another rock rising from the sea and on it a man with a sling is taking aim at the birds which rise scattering this way and that. A boat with a big paddle oar is holding off from the rock, a naked man amidships is giving a queer salute to the slinger, a man kneels over the bows with his back to the others and is letting down a net. The prow of the boat has a beautifully painted eye, so the vessel shall see where it is going. In Syracuse you will see many a two-eyed boat to-day come swimming in to quay. One dolphin is diving down into the sea, one is leaping out. The birds fly, and the garlands hang from the border.

It is all small and gay and quick with life, spontaneous as only young life can be. If only it were not so much damaged, one would be happy, because here is the real Etruscan liveliness and naturalness. It is not impressive or grand. But if you are content with just a sense of the quick ripple of life, then here it is.

The little tomb is empty, save for its shadowy paintings. It has no bed of rock around it: only a deep niche for holding vases, perhaps vases of precious things. The sarcophagus stood on the floor, perhaps under the slinger on the end wall. And it stood alone, for this is an individual tomb, for one person only, as is usual in the older tombs of this necropolis.

In the gable triangle of the end wall, above the slinger and the boat, the space is filled in with one of the frequent Etruscan banqueting scenes of the dead. The dead man, sadly obliterated, reclines upon his banqueting couch with his flat wine-dish in his hand, resting on his elbow, and beside him, also half risen, reclines a handsome and jewelled lady in fine robes, apparently resting her left hand upont he naked breast of the man, and in her right holding up to him the garland—the garland of the female festive offering. Behind the man stands a naked slave-boy, perhaps with music while another naked slave is just filling a wine-jug from a handsome amphora or wine-jar at the side. On the woman's side stands a maiden, apparently playing the flute: for a woman was supposed to play the flute at classic funerals; and beyond sit two maidens with garlands, one turned round to watch the banqueting pair, the other with her back to it all. Beyond the maidens in the corner are more garlands, and two birds, perhaps doves. On the wall behind the head of the banqueting lady is a problematic object, perhaps a bird-cage.

The scene is natural as life, and yet it has a heavy archaic fullness of meaning. It is the death-banquet; and at the same time it is the dead man banqueting in the underworld; for the underworld of the Etruscans was a gay place. While the living feasted out of doors, at the tomb of the dead, the dead himself feasted in like manner, with a lady to offer him garlands and slaves to bring him wine, away in the underworld.

For the life on earth was so good, the life below could but be a continuance of it.

This profound belief in life, acceptance of life, seems characteristic of the Etruscans. It is still vivid in the painted tombs. There is a certain dance and glamour in all the movements, even in those of the naked slave men. They are by no means downtrodden menials; let later Romans say what they will. The slaves in the tombs are surging with full life.

We come up the steps into the upper world, the sea-breeze and the sun. The old dog shambles to his feet, the guide blows out his lamp and locks the gate; we set off again, the dog trundling apathetic at his master's heels, the master speaking to him with the soft Italian familiarity which seems so very different from the spirit of Rome, the strong-willed Latin.

The guide steers across the hilltop, in the clear afternoon sun, towards another little hood of masonry. And one notices there is quite a number of these little gateways, built by the Government to cover the steps that lead down to the separate small tombs. Is it utterly unlike Cerveteri, though the two places are not forty miles apart. Here there is no stately tumulus city, with its highroad between the tombs, and inside, rather noble, many-roomed houses of the dead. Here the little one-room tombs seem scattered at random on the hilltop, here and there: though probably, if excavations were fully carried out, here also we should find a regular city of the dead, with its streets and crossways. And probably each tomb had its little tumulus of piled earth, so that even above-ground there were streets of mounds with tomb entrances. But even so, it would be different from Cerveteri, from Caere; the mounds would be so small, the streets surely irregular. Anyhow, to-day there are scattered little one-room tombs, and we dive down into them just like rabbits popping down a hole. The place is a warren.

It is interesting to find it so different from Cerveteri. The Etruscans carried out perfectly what seems to be the Italian instinct: to have single, independent cities, with a certain surrounding territory, each district speaking its own dialect and feeling at home in its own little capital, yet the whole confederacy of city-states loosely linked together by a common religion and a more-or-less common interest. Even to-day Lucca is very different from Ferrara, and the language is hardly the same. In ancient Etruria this isolation of cities developing according to their own idiosyncrasy, within the loose union of a so-called nation, must have been complete. The contact between the plebs, the mass of the people, of Caere and Tarquinii must have been almost null. They were, no doubt, foreigners to one another.

D. H. Lawrence

"Etruscan Places"

The principal landmarks
in the discovery of Etruscan painting

The publication in 1723-4 of T. Dempster's posthumous "De Etruria regali libri septem" stimulated interest in archaeological investigations. In 1739 a campaign of excavations was started at Volterra and a museum opened in the town.

During the eighteenth century N. Forlivesi was exploring the tombs at Tarquinia. From 1827 systematic excavations were conducted at the same site by J. Micali and Fr. Inghiram.

In 1828-9 Lucien Bonaparte made some sensational discoveries on his estates (jewellery at Ponte Sodo, the Campanari and Isis tombs). Orvieto and Cerveteri (Regolini Galassi tomb), Chiusi, Veii (Campana tomb), Castel d'Asso and Norchia were explored in 1836.

In 1846 Alexandre François discovered the "Monkey tomb" at Chiusi. In the meantime G. Dennis was exploring the whole of Etruria and G. P. Campana, starting in 1850, set on foot several campaigns, discovering amongst others the "Tomb of Reliefs" at Cerveteri.

The most important excavations before 1880, the year when the Italian government initiated large-scale campaigns, took place in 1862 and the following years—the excavations conducted by G. Gozzardini at Marzabotto. 1864 saw the discovery of the "Painted Vases tombs" at Tarquinia, 1868 that of the "Orcus" tomb, 1869 that of "Amazons" sarcophagus and the "Warrior" tomb, 1877 that of the tomb of the "Augurs" and of the "Lionnesses".

Next came the exploration of the necropolis of Tarquinia by G. Ghirardini (from 1881), by A. Pasqui and L. Pernier in 1904-1906 and by G. Cultera fifteen years later.

Saturnia has been excavated by A. Pasqui (1882) and L. Pernier (1918), the necropolis of Vetalonica by I. Falchi (1884) and L. Pernier, who also worked with A. Minto at Orvieto.

Populonia and its vast necropolis was first explored by A. Pasqui (1908) and afterwards (1913 and following years) by G. Giglioli. That of Cerveteri was systematically excavated by R. Menganelli from 1911.

Numerous campaigns are currently in progress, applying to some extent new methods of exploration by drilling.

Prehellenic civilisations

Da-tea	Cretan and Aegean civilisation	Creto-Mycenean civilisation	Historical or Biblical events	Art
	Neolithic			Undecorated but incised pottery. Figurines in terracotta, idols.
)00				
	Eneolithic			
300	First period			
				Monochrome red glaze vases. Geometrical rectilinear motifs.
500				
	EARLY MINOAN			
400				Appearance of curvilinear and spiral motifs. "Fired" style (so-called Vassiliki).
	Second period			
300		PROTO-HELLADIC PERIOD		
200				
	Third Period			Geometrical motifs, discs, chains, spirals, stylised leaves.
100				
)00			Founding of Mycenea, Argos, Tiryns.	
	First period			
900				
	MIDDLE MINOAN			Construction of the first palaces.
800				
	Second period	MIDDLE HELLADIC	Destruction of the first prehellenic palaces.	Phylokopi trescoes. "Crocus gatherer."
700				
	Third period			Camares style. White drawing on black background. Leaves, flowers, rosettes, spirals. First cretan painted frescoes and bas-reliefs. Amnisos frescoes. New palaces.
500		Ancient Mycenean (period of the royal tombs)	The first Hellenes invade Greece. Creto-Mycenean civilisation.	
	First period			
500				"King with fleur de lys" frescoes. "The Bullfight." Polychrome vases, marine subjects, stylised plants, criss-crossing. Frieze of the royal palace at Thebes. Frescoes of the royal palaces at Mycenea and Tyrins. In pottery the "palace" style spreads. Stylised flowers and motifs on mural decorations. Orchomenos and Pylos frescoes.
	LATE MINOAN			
400		(period of the vaulted tombs)	Destruction of the palace of Knossos.	
	Second period			
300		LATE HELLADIC		
			Trojan war. Defeat of the Achaeans in Egypt.	
200	Third period	Late Mycenean (period of vaulted tombs and palaces)		
				Vases decorated with stylised motifs. Appearance of animals, particularly birds. Checked patterns.
100			Dorian invasion.	

Chronology of ancient Greece

Da-tes	Historical or political events	Painting	Pottery
	Beginning of the Iron Age.		
1200			
	Fall of Troy.		
1100	Dorian invasion. Argos, Mycene, Tiryns destroyed.		
	End of the Dorian invasions.		
1000			
900	Formation of the Ionian Confederation.		**Non-Attic geometric style**
			(Rectilinear motifs, zig-zags, meanders, triangles, quadrilles.) Black or reddish brown drawing.)
	HELLENIC MIDDLE AGE	**Geometric period**	
			Thera (Santorin) Boetia.
800	Greek colonial expansion.		
	Cumae first Greek colony in the west. First Messenian war. The Corinthians found Corcyree and Syracuse.		
700	First colonisation of Chalcis by the Eubeans.	**Easternisation of Corinthian Pottery**	**Easternisation of Ionian style**
		a) proto-Corinthian vases	**a) Rhodes:** Camiros and Fykellur style. (Plant and animal decor in black. Figures in opaque silhouet
	Beginning of the Archons in Athens. Second Messenian war.	Black silhouette and incised detail. Favourite form:	**b) Naucratis.** (Scenes with figures. Incision appears, 6th century. Pa colours.) Preferred form: chalice form cups.
	Orthagoras, tyrant of Sicyon. Kypselos, tyrant of Corinth.	Aryballus. "Miniaturist" style, flourished.	
	The Megarians occupy the banks of the Bosphorus.		**c) Clazomenian Pottery.** *Terracotta sarcophagi.* (Black outline drawing on yellowish-whit slip.) *Vases.* (Black silhouettes, made to stand out with red and white touches.) Forms: Elongated amphori, plate, wine cup.
650			
	Cylon conspiracy in Athens. Periander, tyrant of Corinth.		

	Sculpture Architecture	Culture Science	Da-tes
ottery in the proto-geometric style			1200
Circles, semi- and concentric rcles, hatched triangles. Ornaments a central band.)	**From the beginnings to the middle of the sixth century. Decorative statuary and sculpture, geometric and orientalising style. Invention of the basic Kore and Kouros types.**		1100
ecropolis of Thessaly, Phocis, ttica, Peloponnesos, the Aegean, sia Minor.			
			1000
ttic geometric style	Megaron B at Thermos.	Greeks adopt the alphabet.	900
_igh-shade contrast.)			
*rnamented vases. ases with stylised people and nimals. Dipylon vases.			
		Composition of the Homeric lays.	800
ttic black-figured style	Old temple of Artemis Orthia at Sparta.	Seventh and sixth centuries, blossoming of the Ionian cities (Miletus, Ephesus, Clazomenai, Phocaea),to become the economic and cultural centre of Greece. Anchor invented. Terpander writing lyric poetry. Ameinokles of Corinth invents the trireme. Greeks of Asia Minor invent coinage. Poetic career of Archilochos of Paros. Spread of phalanxe tactics in war. Zaleucos, earliest of Greek "legislators". Birth of Sappho.	700
*ainted silhouette, incised detail, •uches of red or white colour.)			
₁vented at Corinth, finds its full ·velopment in Attic art of the ·chaic period.			
	Artemis by Nikander at Delos. Heraion at Olympia.		
	Proto-Attic pottery		650
	(Plant ornament, mythological scenes.)	Tyrtaeos writing poetry. Birth of Thales of Miletus, founder of the Ionian school of philosophy.	
	Analatos hydria. Nessos amphora. Lontiophoroi.		

Da- tes	Historical and political events	Painting	Pottery
600		Kleanthes paints his "Sack of Troy" and "Birth of Athena" at Olympia.	
	Foundation of Massilia (Marseilles).	**b) Corinthian vases**	
		(Black-figured with incisions. Touches of colour for the details. Preference for a single figure.) Shapes: aryballos, alabastron, column krater.	
575			
	Peisistratos, tyrant of Athens.		
550	Formation of the Peloponnesian League.		**d) Caeretan hydria,** metallic type (Yellow or red clay without coating. Incised. Scenes from rea life or mythology.)
	ARCHAIC PERIOD (7th and 6th centuries)		**e) Chalcidian vases.** Euboea, Cumae. (Superb black glaze with bluish reflections. Mu use of incision and touches of
525	Death of Peisistratos.		colour. Ornament in parallel ba Mythological scenes.) **f) Laconian pottery.** Sparta, Cyrene. (Plant and anim motifs. Some mythological subje Colourless slip, numerous fine incisions.) Shape: basin cup.
	Collapse of the tyranny at Athens.		
	Democratic reforms at Athens.		
500	Ionian revolt against the Persians.		
	Destruction of Miletus. End of the Ionian revolt.		
490	**First Persian War.** Battle of Marathon.		
480	**Second Persian War.** Thermopylae. Victories of Salamis and Plataea.		

	Sculpture Architecture	Culture Science	Da-tes
	Temple of Prinias	Draconian code.	600
ttic pottery	Earliest works of Attic statuary (head from Dipylon, Sounion Apollo, Woman from Auxerre (Louvre), Sounion kouros).	Poetry: Alcman. Solon, archon of Athens, reforms the constitution.	
(Mythological subjects, battles.)	Gorgon pediment to the temple of Artemis, Corfu.	Pythian Games take their definitive form.	
ophilos: dinos from the cropolis and Pharsalos. evelopment of black-figured ottery. Dinos from the Acropolis y Lydos. Type of vases called Little Master cups". xekias: emphora of "Ajax and chilles playing dice". anathenian amphorae. Amasis ne painter.	Sphinx from the Naxos treasury, Delphi. **Ionian sculpture predominant.** (Ionian smile, drapery, perfection of the Kouros type, first Acropolis kore.)	Institution of the Nemaean Games. Institution of the Great Panathenian Festivals.	575
	Invention of high-relief. (Friezes, pediments, metopes.)	Death of Solon.	
ed-figured Attic pottery in the evere style.	Moscophoros. Equestrian statues, "Payne-Rampin horse-man".	Anacreon.	550
epresentation of man in his daily fe. Birds, animals and landscapes re forgotten. Realism in anqueting scenes, scenes from the alaestra, mythological subjects. Triumph of drawing. Innovation: reshortening. Drawing of nude gure beneath draperies and ttempt at modelling with help of urvilinear hatchings.) Shapes: ylix, craters. Painters: uphronios, Oltos.	Knidian Treasury at Delphi. Siphnian Treasury at Delphi and frieze.	Institution of the Dionysiac tragedy contest at Athens. Thespis of Icaria, first tragic poet. Birth of Aeschylus. Birth of Pindar.	525
		Rhoikos and Theodoros introduce hollow-casting.	
	Earliest group of Tyrannoctonos statues by Antenor.		
	Stela by Ariston, "Warrior of Marathon", Piombino Apollo. Head of "Fair-headed ephebe", Pouting woman". Pediment to the temple of Eretria. Heraion at Samos.	Heraclitus. Anaxagoras.	500
ase painters: Douris, Makron.	Athenian Treasury at Delphi, metopes. Building of the temple of Poseidon, Sounion. Pediment to the temple of Aphaia at Aegina.	Pericles, 495-429. "Century of Pericles". Flowering of Athenian culture (Aeschylus,	490
	Auriga at Delphi. Tyrannoctonos group by Kritios and Nesiotes.	Sophocles, Euripides, Protagoras, Socrates, Herodotus, Thucydides, Aristophanes).	480

Da-tes	Historical or political events	Painting	Pottery
477	Creation of the League of Delos.		
	Ostracism of Themistocles.		
	Revolt of Naxos against Athens.		
470	Victory of Kimon at the battle of Eurymedon.		
	Pericles, head of the Athenian government.		
	Pre-classical period.		
450	Treasury of Delos transferred to Athens.		
	Formation of the Boeotian Confederation. Thirty Years' Peace between Athens and Sparta.		
	Height of Athenian Power.		
	Peloponnesian War. Plague at Athens. Death of Pericles (429).		
425	Peace concluded by Nikias. Athenian expedition in Sicily meets with disaster. Democracy re-established at Athens.		
	Battle of Aegos Potamoi. Athenian surrender, fleet made over to Lysander, the Long Walls destroyed. Dictatorship of the Thirty. Democracy re-established at Athens.		
400	**CLASSICAL PERIOD** (450-323)		

	Sculpture Architecture	Culture Science	Da-tes
			477
		Pindar at Syracuse.	
		Aeschylus presents "The Persians".	
			470
·d-figured Attic pottery in the ·ssical style ·ses reminiscent of monumental ·inting. Innovations by Polygnotos, ·ecursor of perspective. Scenes of ·mazon contests. Sense of pathos ·d skill in psychological expres-·n. Concurrently, a **school of ·iniaturists** develops. Subjects ·ken from feminine life. Interiors, ·ptial scenes, treated in realistic ·ther than idealistic fashion. ·apes: aryballos-type lekythoi, ·nochoai, pyxides and cups.	Ludovisi triptych. Discobolos and group of Athena and. Marsyas by Myron. Building of the Temple of Zeus at Olympia.	Socrates 469-399. Aeschylus: "Seven against Thebes", "Oresteia". Earliest tragedies by Euripides. Protagoras the sophist starts his career. Birth of the mathematician Theaitetos.	
	Zeus of Histiaca attributed to Kalamis. Pediment of Olympia. Building of the Telesterion at Eleusis. Discophoros, Doryphoros by Polykleitas. Building of the Theseion. Metopes of Slinonte. Statue of Zeus by Pheidias at Olympia. Building of the Parthenon (447-432).	Herodotus at Athens.	450
·e sculptural period succeeded by ·more pictorial style, thanks to ·pollodoros, Zeuxis, Parrhasios, ·ho introduce the play of light ·d shade and perspective effects.	Propylaea. Statue of Athena Parthenos by Pheidias. Panathenian frieze and pediment of the Parthenon. Diadoumenos by Polykleitas.	Pericles in his heyday. The "Antigone" of Sophocles.	
·hite-ground vases ·ps (white slip reserved for the ·edallion, external walls red-·ured). Cups of the potter Sotades. ·kythoi (covered with milky ·ite tone on the belly of the vase. ·ck, handle, base, covered with ·ck glaze). Used mainly for ·nerary purposes.	Victory by Paconios. Temple of Apollo at Bassae from plans drawn by Iktos. Karyatids of the Erectheion at Athens.	The astronomer Meton reforms the calendar. Birth of Hippocrates and Democritus. Birth of Plato.	
		"The Clouds" by Aristophanes.	425
·ttery in regression, though ·aintaining the fifth century ·adition. (Over-loaded composi-·n, frequent touches of white, ·ding.) ·avourite shape: bell krater. ·inters: Eupompos, Pamphilos, ·usias, Euphranor. ·ligious subjects and revival of ·elphic imagery. Predominance of ·onysos and influence of ·uripidean drama. Spina vase, ·phigenia in Tauris".	Hegeso stela.	"Lysistrata" by Aristophanes. "Oedipus Rex" by Sophocles. Meeting between Socrates and Plato. "Iphigenia in Aulis" and "The Bacchac" by Euripides being performed. Death of Sophocles and Euripides.	
		Death of Socrates. Earliest Platonic dialogues.	400

Da-tes	Historical and political events	Painting	Pottery
375	Battle of Leuctra. Sparta loses her supremacy. Battle of Mantinea. Death of Epaminondas. Peace between Thebes, Sparta and Athens. Accession of Philip of Macedon.		
350	End of the third religious war. Amphictionic Peace. Battle of Chaeronea. Lycurgus starts his rule.	Nikomachus paints *The battle of Darius* and the *Abduction of Persephone*.	
336	**Assasination of Philip II.** Accession of Alexander. Alexander in Asia. Battle of Issos. Foundation of Alexandria. Occupation of Babylon, Susa, Persepolis. Alexander campaigns in Central Asia. Alexander recognised by the Greeks as a god. Nuptials of Susa.	Mosaics at Pella, "Lion Hunt".	
323	**Death of Alexander.** Partitition of the satrapies among the diadoukoi. Partition of the empire.	Among the palaces of the Hellenistic kings the most famous are those of Alexandria, decorated with paintings of the school of Sikyon.	**Pottery of the Hellenistic period**
300	Demetrius Poliorcetes reforms the League of Corinth. Battle of Issos. Death of Antigonos. Fresh partition of the empire. Pyrrhos and Lysimachos divide Macedon between them. The Galatians invade Greece. Halted at Delphi.		Imitation of vessels in metal (mot painted in brown, white slip. Ornaments linear or representatio of objects, notably musical instru-ments, animals or plants. Return subjects drawn from nature. Pictorial style in imitation of major painting). Pottery with relief decoration much in fashion. Favourite shape bowls in relief ("Megaran bowls" (Decoration inspired by literature or domestic life.)

	Sculpture Architecture	Culture Science	Dates
		Isocrates: "Panegyric" on Athens.	375
ttery in the so-called "Kertch" le"	Temple of Aesculapios at Epidauros. Destruction of the temple at Delphi. Earliest work by Lysippos.		
lore airy compositions. Plastic ldering of figures. Revival of ʒusinian imagery. New subject: ttle between the Arimaspes and ʒ Gryphons.) Shapes: pelikes, 1ochoai, lekythoi of aryballos ʒe, lekanis, plates decorated with ʒes. inters: Protogenos of Rhodes, ʒelles, Nikias, Nikomachos.	Start made with building the theatre at Epidauros. Temple of Artemis at Ephesus (erected by Croesus) burnt.	Demosthenes: "First Philippic".	
			350
	Praxiteles: "Aphrodite of Knidos" and "Artemis Brauronia".		
	Lysippos working for Alexander. Building of the temple of Athena Polias at Pryene. Choragic monument of Lysikrates.	Demosthenes: "Second Philippic". Aristotle tutor to Alexander. Demosthenes: "Third and Fourth Philippics". Rule of Lycurgos at Athens. Birth of Zeno and Epicuros. Aristotle at Athens, founds the Lyceum. Lycurgos: "Against Leokrates". Demosthenes: "On the Crown".	336
	Completion of the theatre at Epidauros.		
	Temple of Artemis at Sardis.		
			323
		Death of Aristotle. Theophrastos succeeds him at the Lyceum. First comedy by Menander.	
	Choragic monument by Nikias. Victory of Samothrace. Colossos of Rhodes by Chares of Cindos.	Birth of the astronomer Aristarchos of Samos and of Callimachos. Epicurus at Athens. Foundation of the Stoic school. Euclid: "Elements".	300
	Foundation of the museum at Alexandria. Temple of Athena. Palace at Pergamon. Frieze of Pergamon. "Battle of the Giants". Sostratos of Knidos builds the light-house at Alexandria.	Birth of Archimedes of Syracuse.	

Da-tes	Historical and political events	Painting	Pottery
275	**HELLENISTIC PERIOD**		Chief centre of production: Delos
250	Battle of Cleonae.	Painted funerary stelae from Pagasai and Cyprus.	Other workshops: Athens, Boeoti Northern Greece, Asia Minor, Pergamos, Alexandria, Southern Russia.
	Peace of Naupactos.		
200	Alliance between Hannibal and Philip VI. Rome declares war on Philip VI. Flaminius proclaims the freedom of the Greek cities.	Mosaic of the "Battle of Alexander" after a mural painting by Philoxenos of Eretria.	
146	Macedon reduced to a Roman province.		
86	Athens captured by Sulla.		
	Delos and Syracuse pillaged by pirates.		
31	Octavian in Epiros. Battle of Actium.		

Sculpture Architecture	Culture Science	Dates
	Death of Epicuros.	275
	Callimachos: "Hymn to Artemis".	
"The dying Gaul and his wife."		250
Temple of Artemis Leucophryene at Magnesia.	Death of Archimedes. "Septuagint" translation of the Bible.	200
Construction of the Great Altar at Pergamon. "Battle of Attalus against the Gauls" by Epigonos, Phiromachos and Stratonicos.	Library at Pergamon.	146
	Birth of Posidonios of Apamea. Hipparchos of Nicaea discovers the Procession of the Equinoxes.	
		86
"Venus de Milo", probably by Alexander or Agisander of Antioch.		
"Laocoon and his children" by Agisander, Athanadoros and Polydoros of Rhodes.	Library of Alexandria burnt.	31

Etruscan chronology

Dates	Political and historical events	Pottery	Painting	Sculpture
850	Iron Age **Villanovan civilisation** in Tuscany and Latium.			
800				
700	Etruscans arrive in Tuscany.		Tombs of Vetulonia.	
650	Latium occupied by the Etruscans.	Blossoming of "orientalising" civilisation. Difffusion of Proto-Corinthian and Rhodian pottery. Thin Bucchero. Chiusi canopes.	Caere: Tombs of Lions and Painted Animals.	
600	Establishment of Tarquin dynasty at Rome.			Statuary of Vetulonia. "Centaur", "The priestes" Brolio bronzes. Statues of monsters and animals. "Sea horse-man "Lion" (Vulci).
	Foundation of Capua by the Etruscans.	Doric, Corinthian and Ionic influences. Daedalian drawings on vases.		Caere: three terracotta statuettes.
550	Etruscans complete conquest of Etruria.		Bucchero and Campana panels. Chambered tombs appear. Tombs of the Bulls, Inscriptions, Augurs, Lionesses.	
	Capture of Bologna. Etruscans fail before Cumae			
500	Occupation of Rome by the Etruscan Porsenna. Romans win victory of Lake Regilla.	Ionic-Etruscan style at its height. Diffusion of Attic red-figured vases.	Tombs of Hunting and Fishing. Plastic decoration to temple of Veii.	Worked metals at Vulci and Perugia. Terracotta sculpture from the temple of Apollo at Veii. Chiusi reliefs. Terracotta sarcophagi fro Caere.
	First war between Rome and Veii.	Influence of Attic art. Diffusion of Attic red-figured vases in the archaic style. Artistic and cultural heyday of Chiusi.	Tombs of the Lyre-player, the Leopards at Tarquinia. Tombs of Orpheus and Eurydice, of the Monkey, at Chiusi. Veii plaques.	Mirrors appear. Mythological subjects.
475				Hollow seated statues an funerary urns. Sarcophag at Chiusi.

	Historical and political events	Pottery	Painting	Sculpture
	Decadence of the Etruscan world. Second Veian war. Cumae in Samnite hands.	Period of "subarchaism" and influence of Greek pottery, red-figured classical style.	Tarquinia: Tombs of the Triclinium, Funeral Couch, Francesca Giustiniani, Pucella. Chiusi: Tombs of the Hill, Paolozzi.	Bronze statuettes of warriors. "Naked warrior".
)	Conquest of Veii by the Romans. Romans. Reconquest of southern Etruria by the Romans. Forty years' peace between Rome and Tarquinia. Caere beaten by Rome.	Classical influencès enter Etruria from Greece and the Greek cities of southern Italy.		"Arezzo Chimera", "Malavolta head" (Chiusi terracotta). Amazon sarcophagi at Tarquini. "Mars" from Todi.
•			Galini Tomb, Orvieto. Tomb, Tarquinia. Ovcus.	"Ficoroni cist".
	Rome subdues central Etruria.			
)			Tarquinia: Tombs of the Shields, Bruschi, Cardinals. Vulci: Campanari Tomb. Baroque and expressionist tendencies. Hellenistic influences. Apogee of Etruscan por-traiture. François tomb at Vulci. Typhon Tomb at Tarquinii. Decorative and classicising painting. Influences from Pergamon.	Feminine busts from Caere. "Head of Brutus" from the Capitol. Mirrors, chiefly from Praeneste. Scenes from domestic life.
)		Volterra urns.		"Portrait of a man" Bovianum. "Statue of the Arringatore". Sarcophagi sculpted with recumbent figures.
	Under the "Lex Julia" the whole of Etruria annexed to Rome.			

Calendar of Greek archæological discoveries

Archaeological sites	Principal explorations	Principal discoveries and monuments explored
Abdera (Thrace)	Exploration begun in 1950 by the ephor M. D. Lazarides.	Hellenistic walls. Pottery Studios, shops (3rd century B.C.).
Acheron. River of the Dead. (Epiros)	Exploration begun in 1958 by S. Drakasis.	Nekyomanteion (oracle of hades). Statuettes, vases.
Amphipolis. Necropolis (Macedonia)	Systematic explorations from 1956 onward by M. D. Lazarides.	Exploration of 375 tombs (4th and 3rd century B.C.). Vases of the style called Kertch and jewellery.
	Exploration of three tumuli (3rd century B.C.) in 1960.	Three stone beds decorated with frescoes (250-200 B.C.). Jewellery, vases.
Argos (Peloponnesos)	Exploration of the Argive sanctuary consecrated to Hera (Heraion).	
	Expeditions: 1892-1895 by the Am. Sch. of Class. Stud. 1925-1928 by C. W. Blegen. 1947-1949 by P. Amandry of the Fr. Sch. of Athens.	Fragments of the pediment by Polycleitos, metopes.
	Exploration of the Acropolis, of the theatre, and the agora in 1955 by the Fr. Sch. of Athens.	Mosaics from the 4th century B.C.
Athens (Attica)	Extremely vast and numerous explorations. Principal sites explored: all that around the Acropolis, the acropolis itself, the agora, the pottery. Discoveries made on the hill of the Acropolis by the Ephor Cavaddias. Constitutes the most memorable archaeological event of the 19th century. The explorations took place systematically from 1882 onwards. In 1885 the series of Archaic Statues were discovered, later (between 1887-1888) all the innermost recesses of this site were explored, bringing to light, together with numerous statues, vases and diverse objects, several buildings. Recent explorations are mainly due to the Am. Sch. of Class. Stud., begun for the Agora in 1933, and to the archaeological services. In pottery to the Ger. Inst. Arch.	**Acropolis.** Propylaia (437-432). Temple of Athens Nike (after 432-421). Parthenon (447-432). Erechtheion (421-406). In the Acropolis museum: pediments from temples, Cores and Couroi, sculptured plaques of the frieze and fragments of the pediment of the Parthenon. **Areopagus.** Theatre of Dionysous (6th century). Odeon of Herod Atticus. Theseion (449-444). Agora, with numerous monuments from various epochs, cemetery of pottery (tombs of Solon, Pericles, etc., alley of tombs of 4th century). Pottery museum, where one reads about the principal discoveries. Archaeological Museum of Athens possesses the richest collection of vases, statues and other objects of Greek art from various sites in the country.
Bassae. Temple (Peloponnese)	Discovered in 1765 by Bocher. In 1811-1812, the society of "Dilettanti" began explorations and found the 23 plaques of the frieze and metopes bought by the British Museum. It was restored by the Hellenic Archaeological Services.	
Brauron (Attica)	Systematic explorations from 1958 onward. In 1960 the Ephor M. D. Papadimitrion discovered the portico.	Sanctuary of Artemis Brauronia. Tomb thought to be of Iphigeneia.
Corfu (Ionian Iles)	Explorations begun by William II in 1911. Continued by M. Rhomaios in 1925.	Temple of Artemis. Pediment of the Gorgon (about 580 B.C.).
Corinth (Peloponnese)	From 1896, explorations by the Am. Sch. of Class. Stud. Each year continued under direction of H. Robinson. Explorations by Dobstern at Pentesconfi (near Corinth) in 1905. In 1961 trial explorations by Am. Sch. of Class. Stud. at Acrocorinth and Anaploghi.	Cleared the Agora with its principal buildings. Numerous vases. Mosaics of 2nd century B.C., one of which was a picture by Pausias. Discovered fragments of pictures (1,500 other fragments are in the East Berlin Archaeological Museum). Their restoration is in progress. Discovery of the remains of the Sanctuary of Demiter. At Anaploghi narrative mosaic of the 1st century B.C.

rchaeological sites	Principal explorations*	Principal discoveries and monuments explored
rete (Agean Sea)	A merchant of Heraklion, Mr. Kalokairinos, discovers in 1878 the site of Knossos. Systematic explorations were undertaken by Arthur Evans (1900-1905), who brought to light the palace of Minos. Italian archaeologists became interested in Western Crete at the end of the 19th century then, after 1900, through the Ital. Sch. of Athens, they discovered, on the plain of Messara, the palaces of Phaistos and Haghia Triada. The site of Gortyna was first explored by Halbherr, then by an Italian expedition and lastly from 1954 onward by the Ital. Sch. of Athens. Mallia was first explored by J. Hadjidakis (1915) and afterward by the Fr. Sch. of Athens. Hadjidakis also found a princely dwelling at Tylissa, a megaron at Nirou-Chani. Xanthoudidis opened the Tholos tombs of Messara. Explorations of the Ital. Sch. of Athens continue, directed by D. Levi. An important discovery was made by N. Platon at Kato Zacron (1962-1963) of an intact new palace.	Palace of Minos. Frescoes, statuettes. Vases. Inscribed tablets. Palaces of Phaistos and Haghia Triada. Sarcophagus of Haghia Triada. Grotto of Camares: Camares vases. Palace of Maffia. Megaron of Nirou-chari Tomb of Camilari discovered in 1963. Palace of Kato Zacron.
elos (Agean Sea)	Systematic explorations undertaken from 1873 onward by Fr. Sch. of Athens. Continued each year.	Ruins of the ancient city. Sanctuaries of Apollo Delion and Artemis, Porinos Oikos, Italian Agora, theatre. Mosaics from the House of Dolphins and Masks (2nd century B.C.). House of Cleopatra, House of Dionysos (mosaic).
elphi	First explorations undertaken by the architect Laurent (1834). Started again (1840) by O. Müller and E. Curtius, continued by the Fr. Sch. of Athens (1860-1861), exhaustive explorations carried out between 1892 and 1903 by Th. Homolle. R. de Mangol explored the site of Marmaria in 1920. Explorations actively undertaken again about 1935 and P. Amandry Continued them between 1937-1939. They still go on.	Sacred way, various treasures along it (Siphnos, Sicyon, Athemeus). Great temple of Apollo, Theatre gymnasium, Lesche of Cnidos. Hieron of Apollo. Sanctuaries of Athena Pronaia, treasure of Marseilles, gymnasium. In the Museum: "Auriga" of Pythagoras of Samos (474 B.C.). Metopes of the treasure of the Sicyonians (about 560 B.C.), sculptures from the temple of Apollo (end of 6th century), acanthos column (about 400 B.C.).
emetrias (Thessaly)	Explorations undertaken by Ap. Arvanitopoulos in 1914. He discovered here, fitted into the walls of Pagasai, the famous painted stele. Explorations continued by N. Papahatzi.	Today there exist more than 200 stele (2nd century) in the Volos Museum, some of which are painted.
odona	Site identified by Carapanos in 1873. Explorations undertaken again between the wars by Athens Arc. Soc. under the direction of D. Evauphelidis. They continue under the direction of S. Drakakis.	Theatre, sacred house for the oracle cult and ceremonies. Objects placed in Athens Archaeological Museum.
gina (Agean Sea)	Exploration of the Aphaia temple began in 1894 by the Athens Arc. Soc. Carried on by the Ital. Sch. of Athens (1901) under the direction of Mr. Fürtwängler. From 1924 onward a new campaign was under way.	Temple of Aphaia (6th century). Statues found are in the Munich Glyptoteque. Fragments brought to light during explorations can be seen in Aegina Museum and Athens Archaeological Museum.

Archaeological sites	Principal explorations*	Principal discoveries and monuments explored
Eleusis (Attic)	Site was explored by Am. Sch. of Class. Stud. and mainly by the Greek archaeological services directed by J. Travlos. Explorations continue.	Sanctuary of Demeter. Telesterion (initiation hall. A little museum including, amongst other objects, an important collection of pottery from the Mycenean epoch (16th century) up to the red-figured vases of the 5th century.
Epidauros (Argolide)	Initial exploration by the Athens Arc. Soc. (1876-1877) who, on the southern slope of the Acropolis discover the Asculepeion. Between 1881 and 1887 a big campaign led by R. Cavvadias brings to light a large number of diverse buildings relating to the cult of Aesculapios. Fr. Sch. of Athens made explorations in 1946, as did J. Papadimitriou (1948-1951).	Sanctuary of Asclepios. Temples. Tholos. Xenon. Stadium, Theatre. Museum shows various funds related to the cult of Alesculapio remains of pediments and parings.
Eretrea (Euboea)	Explorations from 1900 onward by the Fr. Sch. of Athens taken up again recently.	Ramparts, temple of Apollo Daphnephoros. Gymnasium, Theatre.
Gla (old island of) (Boetia)	Explorations by the Fr. Sch. of Athens from 1883 onwards, lastly continued by J. Threpsiadis.	Remains of a royal residence of the 14th century B.C.
Mycene (Argolida)	The site of Mycene was first explored by Schliemann in 1874-1876. Afterward, successive campaigns were led by Stamatakis (1877-1878), the Athens Arc. Soc. under the direction of Tsountas (1886-1902), Br. Arch. Sch. (1920). Continue after the last war (1952) by the Athens Arc. Soc, directed by J. Papadimitriou, they brought to light, in particular, a second ring of royal tombs.	First ring of royal tombs (16th-15th century) discovered by Schliemann. Lionesses Gate. Cyclopean Walls (1350-1330). Tomb of Clytemnestra (about 1300). Royal Palace (14th century). Citadel. Treasure of Atreus (about 1330). Rich collection of vases. Jewellery, gold objects placed in Athens National Museum. Second royal ring. Recently, discovery of numerous inscribed tablets (linear B).
Olynthos (Macedonia)	First explorations by the Am. Sch. of Class. Stud. directed by Robinson (1928-1938).	The explorations were notable for giving valuable information about Greek town architectur at an older epoch than that of Delos. Of interest, was a tomb of the end of the 5th, beginning of the 4th, century, perfectly preserv with a sealed chamber decorated with painted stucco.
Olympia (Elis)	The first explorations in 1829 by members of the Moree Commission, Blouet and Dubois, fixed the site of the Temple of Zeus and uncovered the three fragments of the Metope (Louvre). Afterward the Germans, directed by Curtius, began an intensive campaign from 1875-1881. Explorations recommenced between 1936 and 1941, directed by Dörpfeld and, after the war, from 1952 onward. They are still continuing.	Gymnasium (Hellenistic epoch). Palestra (end 3rd century). Studio of Pheidias (5th century). Temple of Zeus (468-457). Stadium. Various treasures. The Heraion (end 7th century) where the "Hermes" of Praxiteles was found. The museum reassembles the discoveries made duri explorations, in particular the pediments of the temple of Zeus, the "Victory" of Palionios (befo 420), "Zeus raising Ganymede" (Archaic epoch bronzes and terracottas.
Philippi (Madedonia)	Fr. Sch. of Athens made explorations here as did the Greek Archaeological Services.	Ruins of the city founded by Philip II. Forum two basilicas, Theatre, Agora, Palestra.
Phylakopi (Melos)	Explorations by Br. Arch. Sch.	Brought to light three prehistoric cities. The third (1500-1100) shows the height of Cycladic civilisation. Remains of a palace with numerou frescoes.

Archaeological sites	Principal explorations*	Principal discoveries and monuments explored
Pylos (Triphylia)	Explorations undertaken by Cincinnati University in 1939. Continued from 1952 onwards under the direction of C. W. Blegen.	Palace—probably Nestor's. Important discovery of numerous inscribed tablets (linear B) completing those of Cnossos and the recently discovered ones at Mycene, which permitted Ventris and Chadwick to decipher this language—the ancestor of Greek.
Rhodes (island of)	Numerous explorations by Italian archaeologists during the Italian occupation of this island. Lindos was explored by a Danish team.	**Rhodes.** Stadium. Theatre. Remains of a Temple of Apollo. Temple of Zeus. 4th and 3rd century Necropoleis. **Lindos.** Sanctuary of Athena. **Camiros.** Town with several temples and dwellings. Remains of that of Athena Camiria (6th century).
Samothrace (island of)	Explorations begun by Deville and Cocquart in 1856, continued by Champoixau in 1863; by two expeditions of the Austrian Arch. Inst. (A. Kütze). Systematic exploration by New York University directed by K. Lehmann (1938-1960). They still continue.	Oracle sanctuary of the Cabirois. The "Victory of Samothrace" discovered by Champoixau. Necropolis. Stoa.
Sicyon (Corinthia)	Site was first explored by Am. Sch. of Class. Stud. (1886-1887) and continued by the Athens Arch. Soc.	Gymnasium. Theatre. Small museum includes rich collection of 7th-6th century vases. 4th century mosaics.
Sparta (Laconia)	Various expeditions by Br. Arch. Sch. (1906-1910 and 1924-1928), continued by the Greek Archaeological Services and Athens Arc. Soc. directed by Chr. Christou.	Acropolis. Ruins of temple of Artemis Orthia. Mosaics from Roman villas. Explorations showed existence in Laconia of studios producing "Laconian Pottery".
Tanagra (Boetia)	Explorations undertaken by Athens Arc. Soc. (1873, 1875, 1876), continued in 1880 by Fr. Sch. of Athens.	Necropolis. Nearly five thousand tombs were opened. Statuettes.
Thebes (Boetia)	Explorations by Fr. Sch. of Athens in 1890 and 1899 then by Athens Arc. Soc. directed by A. Keramopoulos (1910), continued in 1963 by Greek Archaeological Services directed by N. Plato.	Palace of Kadmos (circa 1450-1350) exhumed by A. Kermapoulos also Ismenion or temple of Apollo Ismenios. Ruins of the antique city. Palace treasure discovered in 1963 with remains of frescoes and important collection of rings.
Thermou (Etolia)	Explored by the Athens Arc. Soc. in 1897-1916 then in 1924 and in 1931-1932.	Federal Sanctuary of the Etolian League of Apollo Thermios (6th century). Site of painted tiles.
Tiryus (Argolid)	Systematic explorations by Schliemann and Dörpfeld in 1884-1885, continued by Dörpfeld and Karo in 1905, by Karo, Küntze and Müller in 1926-1927.	Cyclopean Walls. Megaron (circa 1400). Important remains of frescoes found in the palace (National Museum of Athens).

* Abbreviations

Am. Sch. of Class. Stud.	American School of Classical Studies	Ger. Inst. Arch.	German Institute of Archaeology
Fr. Sch. of Athens	French School of Athens	Br. Arch. Sch.	British School of Archaeology
Athens Arc. Soc.	Athens Archaeological Society	Ital. Sch. of Athens	Italian School of Athens.

Alabastron
Cylindrical shape, mouth narrow with wide borders.

Amphora
Two-handled, pot-bellied, used for keeping food and liquids. Together with the cup, the Attic vase *par excellence*.

Aryballos, globular and pear-shaped
Perfume vases. They have a narrow mouth with wide borders which allows the perfume to be sprinkled on the skin. They belong specifically to Corinthian pottery.

Askos
A curved shape, simulating bottles made of skin.

Cup
Used for drinking. A great variety of shapes.

Dinos
Vase in the form of a cauldron balanced on a moulded support. No handles. Type very widespread in the archaic period. Survived until the end of the fifth century B.C.

Epinetron or onos
Instrument used in spinning wool, whose decoration has affinity with that of the vases.

Hydria
Huge vase for water, relatively narrow-mouthed. Has three handles, one large vertical one for carrying by and two small lateral ones for pouring out the contents. Vases of this type are found from the archaic period down to the end of the fourth century B.C.

Kantharos
Drinking vase in clay or metal, as a rule richly decorated and bearing incisions.

Krater
Large vase for mixing water and wine.

Column Krater
Pot-bellied vase having handles in the form of cylindrical shafts which terminate as a horizontal appendix. Very widespread in the sixth century B.C.

Volute krater
Owes its name to the form of the handles. Continues down to the end of the fifth century B.C.

135

Calyx krater
Has a belly in the form of a calyx which broadens out at the top. The two handles are placed at the base of the Calýx.

Bell krater
In the form of an inverted bell. The handles are at the top of the body.

Lagynos
In the form of our modern carafe.

Lebes gamikos
Almost the same shape as the dinos, but with two double handles at the top of the shoulder. Used in nuptial ceremonies.

Lekythos
Funerary vase, very common in the archaic period.

Squat lekythos
Same type as the above, but squatter. It has a white slip coating and was very widespread in the fifth century.

Lekane
Variant of the preceding type with two strong handles and a cover.

Loutrophoros
Spindle-shaped with two fairly thin handles. Used in nuptial ceremonies at Athens, to carry water from the Kallirhoe fountain for the bride's bath. Also placed on tombs of the unmarried.

Oinochoe
Used as a decanter, i.e. wine was drawn into it from another receptacle and then poured into the cups of the guests.

Pelike
Pot-bellied, two-handled, broadening towards the base. Very like an amphora. Appears at Athens towards the end of the sixth century B.C. and towards the end of the fourth century takes over from the amphora.

Pithos
Large vase in the shape of a jar, ovoid, in which oil or cereals were kept, hence the large number of them found in the cellars of houses.

Phiale
Drinking vase with multiple variants.

Psykter
(Psykter is derived from the Greek word for cold.) It is thought the ancients filled it with cold water and then plunged it in a krater to refresh the wine before a feast. Top-shaped.

Pyxis
A king of cosmetic box, many different forms.

Skyphos
Like the cup, kanthar and phiale, a drinking vase. This too has many variants.

Stamnos
Quite large, pot-bellied, with two small horizontal handles and a relatively narrow mouth. Used for keeping wine.

List of Museums

Greek Painting

Museum at Argos
Akropolis Museum, Athens
Agora Museum, Athens
Kerameikos Museum, Athens
National Museum, Athens
Staatliche Museen, Berlin
Museum of Antiquities, Bologna
Museum of Fine Arts, Boston
Musées Royaux du Cinquantenaire, Brussels
Museum at Corinth
Archaeological Museum at Heraklion, Crete
Museum at Eleusis
Museo Archeologico, Florence
Rijksmuseum van Oudheden, Leyden
British Museum, London
Staatliche Antikensammlungen, Munich
Museo Nazionale, Naples
Metropolitan Museum of Art, New York
Museo Nazionale, Palermo
Cabinet des médailles, Paris
Louvre, Paris
Museo nazionale di villa Giulia, Rome
Museo nazionale, Tarentum
Gregorian Museum, Vatican
Kunsthistorisches Museum, Vienna
Museum at Volos
Martin von Wagner Museum, Würzburg

Orvieto:	Golini Tomb
Tarquinia:	Tomb of Inscriptions
	Tomb of the Augurs
	Tomb of the Dead Man
	Tomb of the Lionesses
	Tomb of Hunting and Fishing
	Tomb of the Bacchantes
	Tomb of the Old Man and the Vases
	Tomb of the Baron
	Tomb of the Dying Man
	Tomb of the Chariots
	Tomb of the Lyre-Player
	Tomb of the Leopards
	Tomb of the Triclinium
	Tomb of the Funeral Couch
	Tomb Francesca Giustiniani
	Tomb of Querciola
	Tomb of the Pulcella
	Sarcophagus of the Amazons
	Tomb of Orcus
	Tomb of the Shields
	Tomb of Bruschi
	Tomb of the Cardinal
	Tomb of the Typhon
Veii:	Campana Tomb
	Veii plaques
Vulci:	Campanari Tomb
	François Tomb

Etruscan Painting

Principal monuments with painting

Cerveteri:	Tombs of the Lions and
	Tomb of the Animals
	Boccanera plaques
	Campana plaques
Chiusi:	Tomb of the Monkey
	Tomb of the Hill
	Paolozzi Tomb
	Tomb of Orpheus and Eurydice

Museums

Antiquarium, Berlin
Museum of Antiquities, Bologna
Museo Civico, Chiusi
Museo Archeologico, Florence
British Museum, London
Museo del Opera, Orvieto
Museo Nazionale, Palermo
Louvre, Paris
Museo nazionale di villa Giulia, Rome
Museum at Tarquinia
Etruscan Museum, Vatican
Kunsthistorisches Museum, Vienna
Museum at Volterra

139

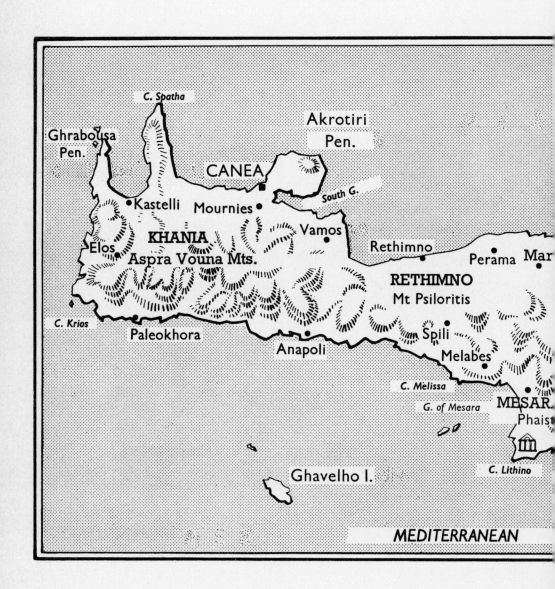

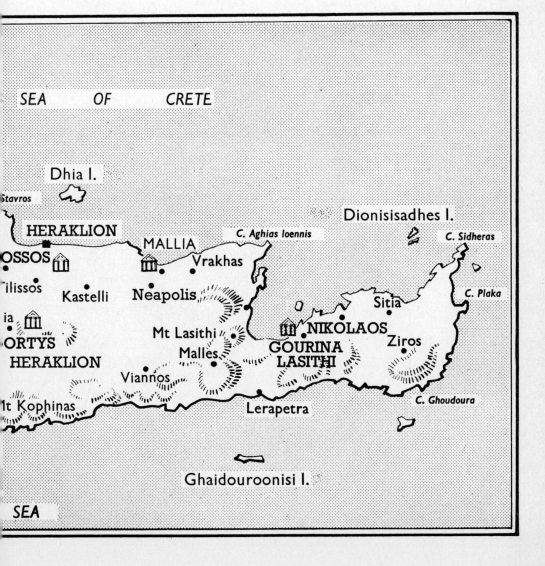

SEA OF CRETE

Dhia I.

Stavros

HERAKLION

OSSOS

Tilissos

Kastelli

ia

**ORTYS
HERAKLION**

1t Kophinas

MALLIA

Vrakhas

Neapolis

Mt Lasithi

Malles

Viannos

Dionisisadhes I.

C. Aghias Ioennis

C. Sidheras

C. Plaka

Sitia

**NIKOLAOS
GOURINA
LASITHI**

Ziros

Lerapetra

C. Ghoudoura

Ghaidouroonisi I.

SEA

141

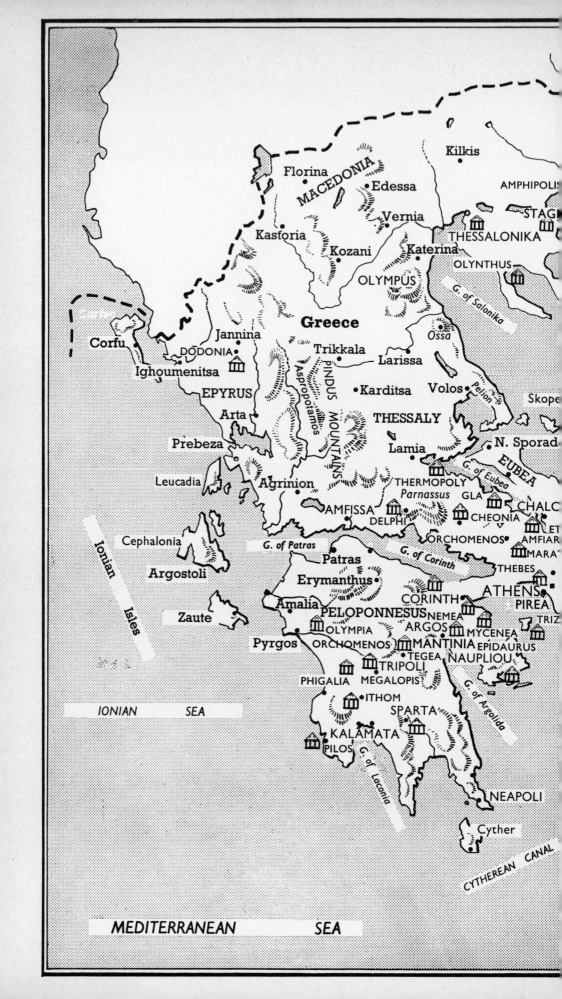

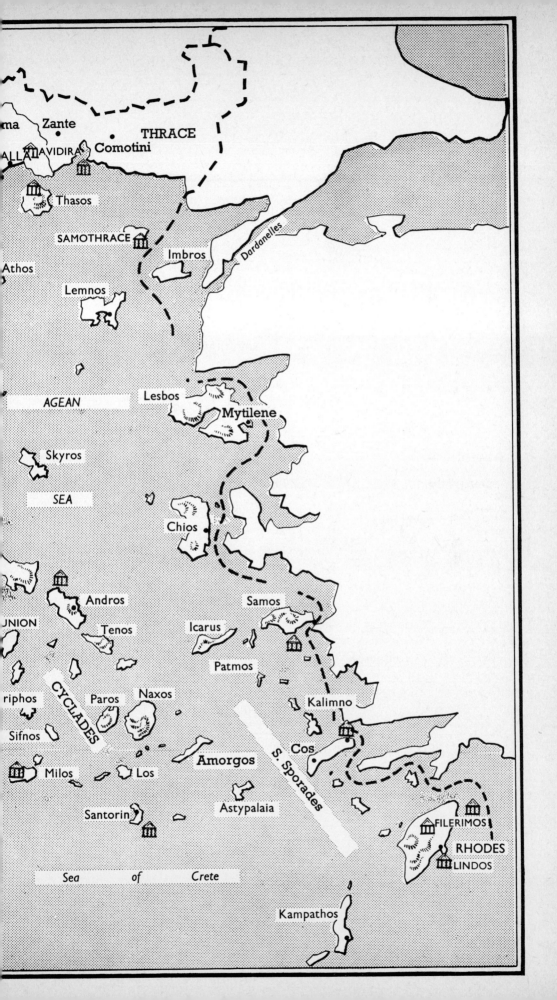

Etruria

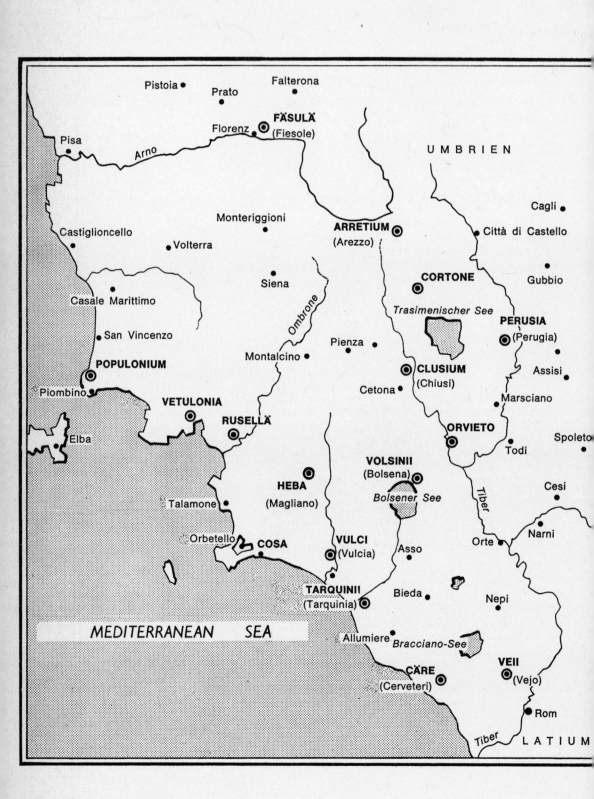

Pistoia

Prato

Falterona

FÄSULÄ
(Fiesole)

Florenz

Pisa

Arno

UMBRIEN

Monteriggioni

Cagli

ARRETIUM
(Arezzo)

Città di Castello

Castiglioncello

Volterra

CORTONE

Gubbio

Siena

Trasimenischer See

PERUSIA
(Perugia)

Casale Marittimo

Ombrone

Pienza

Assisi

San Vincenzo

Montalcino

CLUSIUM
(Chiusi)

Marsciano

POPULONIUM

Cetona

Piombino

VETULONIA

ORVIETO

Spoleto

Elba

RUSELLÄ

Todi

VOLSINII
(Bolsena)

Cesi

HEBA
(Magliano)

Bolsener See

Talamone

Tiber

Narni

Orbetello

COSA

VULCI
(Vulcia)

Asso

Orte

TARQUINII
(Tarquinia)

Bieda

Nepi

MEDITERRANEAN   SEA

Allumiere

Bracciano-See

VEII
(Vejo)

CÄRE
(Cerveteri)

Rom

Tiber

LATIUM

Dictionary

Acropolis

Name given to the upper town of ancient Greek cities. Standing usually on an escarpment and protected from surprise attack by its natural situation, the acropolis was further defended by a fortified enclosure, which in time of danger gave shelter to the inhabitants of the lower town. In most cities the enclosure also contained the temples dedicated to the tutelary deities. The acropolis was thus not only a citadel but also a sanctuary, guardian of traditions and object of veneration to the people scattered on its flanks and at its feet. There was an acropolis in a very large number of the Greek cities and of the Greek colonies in Asia Minor, Sicily and Italy. The name Acropolis is more specifically applied to that of Athens, the most beautiful of all and the richest both in monuments and associations, in short the acropolis *par excellence*. A centre as much religious as political, placed under the protection of Minerva, tutelary goddess of the Athenians, it was from an early date covered with magnificent monuments. The chief buildings to visit are the Propylaea, the temple of Nike Apteros (Wing-less Victory), the Erectheion and, in the centre, the Parthenon. Other famous examples of an acropolis whose ruins are still extant include those of Mycenae, Tiryns, Corinth, Lykosoura, Orchomenos and Messina.

Aegean

Name given by the Greeks to the sea which washes the Attic coastline, in memory of king Aegeus, father of Theseus, who allegedly threw himself into it. Its principal groups of islands are the Sporades and the Cyclades.

Aeschylus

The earliest of the three great tragic poets of Greece. He was born at Eleusis in 525 B.C. and died at Gela in Sicily in 456. He fought at Marathon, at Salamis and Plataea and drew his initial inspiration from the patriotic sentiment stimulated by war. Having won great renown for his plays, he left Athens for Sicily, probably in 469. An anecdote recounted by the Elder Pliny ascribes his death to a tortoise dropped on his bald head by an eagle. Aeschylus added much to the paraphernalia of the decor and scenic effect. He invented the tragic mask and mantle, supplementing them by the cothurnus; he introduced a second actor in addition to the sole performer who formerly came on to make a speech between two choral passages, thus relegating the choir to second place and making dialogue the principal object of tragedy. Finally he conferred a sustained nobility and modesty on the tragic style. His characters are often legendary heroes and the whole action is dominated by the tragic sense of destiny.

Aetolia

Territory of ancient Greece, west of Attica, towards the Ionian sea. The principal towns were Naupactos, Calydon, Thermos. The Aetolians, brigands and pirates, formed a league which was important in the later days of Greece. It was directed by a strategos, a general assembly, judges, a secretary of state, ephors. Victorious over Aratos and the Achaeans at Caphyes, the Aetolians allied with the Romans against Macedon, then summoned Antiochus to Greece and were reduced by Fulvius Nobilor.

Agatharcos of Samos

(Second half of the fifth century B.C.) Artist contemporary with Zeuxis. He studied more deeply the problems of representing space, to which Polygnotus and Mikon had already made a fundamental contribution, and invented a new style of painting which marked a great advance in art, particularly as regards landscape and architectural decoration. Agatharcos began as a mural artist, for we know that he decorated the house of Alcibiades; afterwards he painted the first theatrical decors, perhaps at the suggestion of Aeschylus. The painter truly created the "scene", to use the ancient expression, that is he represented the buildings demanded by the action. This

type of work suited his great talent for improvisation. These works contained a first attempt at diminishing lines to give the illusion of depth. Agatharcos of Samos therefore passes as the inventor of perspective, whose effect he sought to accentuate by the play of shade and light and special colour contrasts.

Aghelades of Argos

Sculptor who brought to life the school of Argos, at the end of the sixth and the beginning of the fifth century B.C. The ancients regarded him as the master of Polykleitos and also number Pheidias and Myron among his pupils. Agheladas was the author of numerous statues of athletes in bronze, many of which were displayed in the sanctuary at Olympia. He also made effigies of gods, notably the Zeus Ithomatas, set up on the ancient holy mountain of Messenia, and the prophylactic Herakles, which was consecrated by the Athenians in the dome of Melite, during the great Attic plague of 430.

Agora

The great square where the citizens gathered to hold their political assemblies On other days it served as a market and a place for strolling about and meeting people. Always situated in the lower town, it took the form of a rectangle surrounded by monumental buildings, among which figured several porticoes (stoa) which served as a shelter from sun and rain. Every Greek city possessed its

147

agora, of greater or lesser dimensions, in which during certain hours of the day the life of the city was concentrated.

Aison

Greek painter who worked towards the end of the fifth century B.C. Contemporary of Meidias the potter. He painted a considerable number of white-ground lekythoi. His most celebrated work is the vase on which the "seven exploits of Theseus" are depicted (Madrid, Archaeological Museum).

Alcibiades

(450?-404 B.C.) Athenian general, nephew of Pericles and disciple of Socrates. Rich, educated, he was the most brilliant man of his time. He reflects its qualities and its defects, its splendours and miseries, its vast political and intellectual aspirations as they conflicted with the thirst for pleasure and uncertainty about the future. Few men have united in themselves such contrasts, few have lived so turbulent a life as Alcibiades. He dragged his country into the disastrous expedition against Sicily in 415. During the Peloponnesian war he served and betrayed Athens by turns. Taking refuge first in Sparta and then in Asia Minor, he exerted himself on behalf of his native city and regained power, to be deprived of it again in 407. He died in exile, assassinated by order of Pharnatesos, satrap of Bithynia.

Alexander the Great

King of Macedon, son of Philip, pupil of Aristotle, he was born in 356 B.C. and came to the throne in 336. Having subjected Greece, he decreed for himself the title of generalissimo of the Hellenes against the Persians, crossed the Hellespont at the head of 40,000 men and defeated the troops of Darius at the Granicus (334) and at Issos (333), took Tyre, Sidon etc., conquered Egypt where he founded Alexandria. Next, crossing the Tigris and Euphrates, he won his decisive victory over the Persians at Arbela (331) Continuing his march, he took Babylon, Susa and Persepolis and pressed on as far as the Indus. He returned to Babylon because his army refused to go any further and died there of an acute fever at the age of thirty-three (323 B.C.). He is one of the three or four men whose exploits have most

Fight against the Amazons
Magnesia on the Meander
Paris, Louvre

excited the admiration of the European peoples. The work he accomplished opened a new era in the history of the Mediterranean world. Alexander is the most powerful personality to have left his mark on this history.

Alexandria

City in Lower Egypt, founded in 332 B.C. by Alexander the Great. Magnificent monuments, for example the lighthouse, considered one of the seven wonders of the world, rapidly made Alexandria a most marvellous city. Its admirable commercial situation brought it an unprecedented degree of prosperity. During the Hellenistic and Roman periods it was the entrepot for the riches of the East and the most important port in the Mediterranean. The Lagid Ptolemies, successors of Alexander, also made Alexandria the intellectual capital of the known world. The Museum included a famous library of 700,000 volumes, collected together from all countries of the world (it was burnt in 47 B.C. when Julius Caesar burnt the Alexandrian fleet stationed in the harbour). Alexandria became the chosen meeting-place for scholars and artists of the day. The last of the great philosophical schools of antiquity originated here and bears its name. Its teaching, largely a rejuvenated form of Platonism, attempts to reconcile the Greek spirit with Oriental thought. The most famous work to issue from this school was "The Enneads" of Plotinus.

Amasis

Potter and painter of the mid-sixth century B.C. who for some unknown reason bears the hellenised name of two Egyptian Pharaohs. The city in which he worked is unknown. The inscriptions on his vases are in Attic script, yet among the shapes he affects is the Doric olpe. He is somewhat formalist in style. Only nine vases signed by him are known. The two finest are in the Cabinet de Medailles, Bibliothèque Nationale (decoration: warriors in combat, Athena and Poseidon, Dionysos and the Menads) and the Louvre (decoration: Athena, Poseidon, Hermes and Herakles).

Amazons

Mythical race of female warriors. Their country has been placed on the shores of the Black Sea. Daughters and priestesses of a lunar divinity identified with Artemis, they hated men, whom they admitted to their company only once a year. Their male children were either massacred or sent back to their own countries. The girls underwent excision of the right breast to make it easier to draw a bow. The two most famous Amazon contests were the battle between the Amazons and Herakles, whose ninth labour was to

149

capture the girdle of Ares from Hippolyta, their queen, and the famous exploit of Theseus in abducting their queen Antiope from her court. In reprisal the Amazons invaded the territory of Athens and penetrated the city. A favourite subject with sculptors, often taken up by vase painters. Mention should also be made of the lost paintings by Mikon and Polygnotos in the Poikile and in the temple of Theseus at Athens.

Amphiaraos

Corinthian painter potter of the early sixth century B.C.

Anaxagoras of Clazomenai

(499 ?-428 B.C.) Greek philosopher of the Ionian school, born in Asia minor. Belonging by birth to a rich and powerful family, he had leisure to devote himself to the study of philosophy and astronomy. At the age of twenty he came to Athens, became the friend of Pericles and had Euripides, Archelaus and perhaps Socrates as his pupils. He is regarded as the founder of philosophic theism.

Anchermos

Greek sculptor of the archaic period, native of Chios. Worked at Delos during the first part. of the sixth century. We learn from a speech by the scholiast in the "Birds" of Aristophanes that he was the first to give wings to Nike, goddess of victory.

Andokides

One of the earliest Athenian potters (third quarter of the sixth century B.C.) to practise the black-figured and red-figured technique concurrently. It has even been suggested that he invented the latter, reversing the old method, as it were, by making the ground black and reserving the colour of the red clay for the figures.

Antioch

Syrian city on the Orontes, founded 301 B.C. Residence of the Seleucids and capital of Syria, it was for centuries one of the chief cities of the world. In the Hellenistic period it numbered more than 50,000 inhabitants and was famous for its wealth, magnificence and luxury, to which important ruins of rich mansions, adorned with remarkable mosaics, bear witness.

Apelles

One of the greatest painters of Antiquity. According to Pliny, he surpassed all his predecessors and none who came later could equal him. He was born at Colophon and resided at Ephesus (fourth century B.C.). He was active between 350 and 320 B.C. About 340 he was living at the court of Alexander the Great and became his official painter. He made several portraits of the great conqueror (one adorned the temple of Artemis at Ephesus) and of notables of his court. In the latter part of his career he seems to have concentrated mainly on mythological paintings. He made a fairly prolonged stay in Alexandria, where he composed his great allegorical picture *Calumny*, described by Lucian, which a number of sixteenth and seventeenth painters (for example, Dürer and Botticelli) attempted to reproduce. He seems to have finished his days on the island of Cos, at the time when he was working on his picture of *Aphrodite Anadyomene*, inspired by the courtesan Phryne; of all his works, this was the most admired by the Ancients. His other mythological pictures included a *Seated Psyche*, *Artemis hunting with her companions*, *Herakles*, *Naked Eros*, personifications of natural forces, etc.

Apollodoros of Athens

Painter contemporary with Zeuxis (fifth century B.C.). He had a great influence on the painting of his day since he was the first to discover how to give relief to figures by a graduation of shadows and colours and by taking advantage of the projected shadow. (Plutarch says he "proceeded by graduated and diminished tones".) He departed from the fresco painting of his predecessors and painted on wooden tablets, using water mixed with egg yolk. Pliny refers to his *Priest at prayer* and *Ajax smitten by the thunderbolt* and adds that he also painted "monochromes in white".

Archelaos

King of Macedon from 413 to 399 B.C., famous in particular for his encouragement of the arts. Fascinated by Hellenic culture, he was eager to transplant its most brilliant manifestations to his court, and succeeded in attracting the poets Choerilos and Agathon. When Euripides was banished he found asylum with Archelaos and celebrated his fame in a lost tragedy, *Archelaos*. Zeuxis decorated his palace with paintings. He founded games in honour of Zeus and the Muses in the city of Dion.

Argos

Ancient capital of the Argolid in the north-eastern Peloponnesos, close to the gulf of Nauplion. Its origins are lost in the mists of time and the city is associated with many stories of Greek mythology. After the Dorian invasion it became one of the principal cities of the Peloponnesos and the rival of Sparta. The Argives claimed to be the most ancient people in Greece. They had a passion for gymnastic games. Argos was a great artistic centre and its school of sculpture produced the four great masters, Agheladas, Miron, Pheidias and Polykleitas.

151

Aridikes of Corinth

(Seventh century B.C.) Contemporary of Kleanthes whose experiments he emulated, in that he always worked in a single colour. But the advance for which he and his other contemporary Telephanes of Sikyon have received the credit was that of tracing lines within the dark silhouette of these monochromes, lines which by setting off the members of the trunk and emphasising their movement would give some idea of the modelling of the body.

Arigontos

Corinthian artist of the seventh century B.C. Strabo attributes to him an *Artemis riding on a gryphon* to be found at the Alpheionia temple near Olympia.

Aristeides

In the present state of our knowledge it is difficult to make a clear distinction between the two painters known as Aristeides the Elder and Aristeides the Younger. Pliny is responsible for this confusion. He identified the two Aristeides, one living in the first half of the fourth century and the other in the time of Alexander, who may have been the grandson of the former. It is the younger Aristeides who is supposed to have composed a *Battle between the Greeks and the Persians*, containing nearly a hundred people, and painted the *Portrait of Leontion*, mistress of Epicurus. Pliny associates Aristeides of Thebes in Boeotia with the invention of encaustic painting and credits him with the discovery of ways to express the soul.

Aristophanes

(Athens, 450-386 B.C.) The most celebrated of the Greek comic poets. His life is very obscure. Nothing is known of his origin, which was probably non-Athenian and perhaps even non-Greek (some have claimed he was Egyptian). We are equally ignorant concerning his education. He wrote fifty-four plays, the majority of them known only from fragments. Only eleven have come down to us complete.

Aristotle

(384-322 B.C.) Famous Greek philosopher born at Stagira in Macedon; he died at Chalcis in the Euboea. He spent twenty years as a pupil of Plato. He was tutor to Alexander the Great and founded the Peripatetic school. One of the greatest minds of all time, he was the first to make a systematic study of all the disciplines, not only philosophical but also scientific. He looked for a way round

the Platonic dualism which contrasted material reality with ideas. His metaphysic can be defined as a system of development in which matter and form are inseparable elements. Aristotle discovered an incomparable instrument for philosophical method, a universal procedure of analysis and demonstration: logic. For the axion of the Platonic school "Let no one enter here who is not a geometer" he substituted: "Let no one enter here who is not a logican".

Artemis, Temple of at Ephesus

According to the ancient authorities it was founded by the Amazons. Pliny reports that the temple was sacked seven times. After the invasion of the Cimmerians in the seventh century B.C. it was rebuilt by Croesus, king of Lydia, and its splendour dates from this epoch. In 356 B.C. a madman named Herostratos, to give immortality to his name, set fire to the Temple, on the very night Alexander the Great was born. The Ephesians had him tortured and forbade anyone on pain of death to pronounce his name, which has nevertheless been preserved by the historians.

Athens

Principal city of ancient Greece. Capital of modern Greece. By reason of its wealth, civilisation, power and political importance it was one of the most flourishing cities of Antiquity. It was the homeland of Plato, Euripides, Aristophanes, Aeschylus, Sophocles, Thucydides, Pheidias, Pericles, Demosthenes, etc. The most celebrated monuments surviving on the Acropolis are: the Propylaea, the Parthenon, the Erechtheion, the temple of Athena Nike. In the lower town: the Agora, Kerameikos, the Theseion, the theatre of Dionysos, the monument of Lysicrates. The Odeion of Herodes Atticus and the Library of Hadrian date from the Roman period.

Attica

Territory of ancient Greece situated to the north-east of the Peloponnese, lying between the Aegean sea, Megara and Boeotia, whose capital was Athens. The principal ancient cities were Eleusis, Piraeos, Phyle, Marathon and Oenoe.

153

Boeotia

Territory of ancient Greece, whose capital was Thebes. Boeotia was situated to the south of Phocis and Locris. The principal Boeotian cities formed a confederation called the Boeotian League, whose twelve chiefs called themselves the Boeotarchs. Boetia gave birth to Hesiod, Plutarch, Pelopidas, Pindar, Epaminondas and Corinna.

Bosphoros

Name given by the Greeks to the strait which links the Black Sea with the Sea of Marmora, subsequently applied to the strait which unites the Black Sea with the Sea of Azov; the first was the Thracian Bosphoros which we still call the Bosphoros or channel of Constantinople; the second was the Cimmerian Bosphorus. The etymology of the word Bosphorus—ox passage—is connected with the legend of Io, who was supposed to have swum across the sea at this point in the form of a heifer.

Boularchos

Ionian painter of the late eight century. He must have painted large pictures, among them *The battle in the valley of the Maeander*, fought by the Magnesians with fighting dogs against some enemies unknown. Pliny, who mentions this work,

adds that it was acquired by Candaules, king of Lydia.

Bouleterion

Meeting-hall of the "boule" or senate of a Greek city.

Boupalos of Chios

(Second half of the sixth century B.C.) Sculptor, son of Archermos and brother of Athenis. He worked with his brother at Delos and in several cities of Asia Minor. They made statues of Artemis for Lasos (Crete) and Chios, their homeland. Pausanias cites a statue at Smyrna of Fortune wearing the "polos" on her head and holding the horn of Amalthea. He seems to imply that Boupalos was the creator of this type, which became classic. Again according to Pausanias, Boupalos was also an architect. When the Romans became art-lovers, the two sons of Archermos enjoyed their favour. Augustus had a fondness for these artists and had some of their works placed in the temple of Apollo on the Palatine.

Brygos

(First third of the fifth century.) Highly talented painter, contemporary of Douris, who had his studio in Athens. Many of his cups have come down to us. One of the most beautiful, decorated with the

Brygos cup, first quarter of 5th century
Sack of Troy (detail from the interior)
Paris, Louvre

"Massacre of the sons of Priam" is in the Louvre. His taste was in the direction of large epic compositions. He pressages the classical style and aims at dramatic effect. He was prodigal with gold in painting.

Busiris

Fabled king of Egypt. All strangers who entered his kingdom were sacrificed on the altar of his gods. He continued this slaughter until the day when Herakles, brought to Egypt on his errand to pick the golden apples, was captured by the king's myrmidons. He allowed himself to be led to the altar but there burst his bonds and slew both the priests and the tyrant. The scene is represented in numerous vase paintings.

Calydon

City of Oenos and Tydeos to the north of Laphrion, in Aetolia. It was close to the forest in which Meleager killed the famous boar sent by Diana to ravage the countryside, a legend recounted by Ovid in the eighth book of his *Metamorphoses*.

Candaules

Legendary king of Lydia. Last of the Heraklides. According to Herodotos, this monarch, very proud of the beauty of his wife Nyssia, made her expose herself to Gyges, his favourite. She became aware of his presence, forced Gyges to kill her husband and to take his place. In another version of the legend, told by Plato, Gyges was a simple Lydian herdsman who found a magic ring: he had only to turn the stone inside to become invisible. By this means he seduced the queen and assassinated king Candaules.

Canopics

In Egypt, earthenware vases with a lid in the form of a god's head. They were arranged in groups of four near the mummies and held the viscera of the dead, separately embalmed. By analogy, the same term is used for a particular type of Etruscan ceinerary urn, made of terracotta or bronze. The urn takes the form of an ovoid pot and has as its lid a human head, whose neck plugs the aper-

155

Canopic vase with bronze base
Terracotta head with gold ear-rings
7th and 6th century B.C.
Chiusi, Etruscan Museum

Pediment of the temple of Zeus
Centaur struggling with Lapiths
Olympia Museum

ture of the vessel. These heads, of a powerful realism, seem to have been executed from a death mask taken on the body. The Etruscan canopics are usually pierced by two or three holes at the top, since it was believed it was essential to allow egress to the spirits and thus permit them to continue in communion with the living.

Capua

Ancient city of Campania, founded in 856 B.C. It allied with Hannibal and was conquered by Rome in 211 B.C. It was the most famous pleasure resort in Italy. It is said that Hannibal's army, resting there after the battle of Cannae, was enervated through succumbing to its delights. Hence the proverbial expression "the delights of Capua", signifying enjoyment and relaxation which deprives one of energy.

Carthage

Important city of ancient Africa, situated in the recess of a large bay. It was founded in the seventh century B.C. by the Phoenicians. Protected by huge walled fortifications, it comprised the citadel of Byrsa, the new city, or Megara, and two harbours, one for ships of war, the other for merchant ships. Defeated by Rome in the three Punic wars, it was destroyed by Scipio in 146 B.C. Rebuilt first by C. Gracchus and then by Augustus, under the emperors it was again a flourishing city. The Muslim invasion put an end to its existence: in 698 it was sacked by Hassan the Gassanid.

Cella (or Naos)

One of the three large interior divisions of an ancient temple. In early temples the cella constituted the whole. Later new chambers were added: the pronaos, opisthodomos and peristyle. Shields were fixed to the columns and walls; votive tables and works of art stood on the marble pavement.

Centaurs

Fabulous beings, half men and half horse, who inhabited the mountains of Pelion and Ossa in Thessaly. As a rule they were malevolent and brutal. Herakles had to give battle to the Centaurs as one of his twelve labours. Another of their battles was against the Lapiths, on the occasion of the marriage between Pirithoos and Hippodamia. In the midst of the feasting they tried to carry off the bride and set about ravishing the women. This was a favourite subject with ancient sculptors and poets.

Cerveteri (Caere)

Etrurian city founded in the eighth century B.C. and which flourished for several centuries. It was the headquarters of one of the twelve lucumonies of Etruria. In 351 the city became subject to Rome. It was from Caere, it seems, that the Romans gained their knowledge of the Etruscan mysteries or religious rites and also of the art of sacrificing; the word "ceremony" is allegedly derived from Caere. Several large Etruscan necropoleis with tumulus graves have been found in the vicinity. Excavations started in 1911. The most interesting tombs are those of the Lions, the Shields, and the Sarcophagi. A number of vases in the Graeco-Oriental style have been found there, also the famous "Boccanera" and "Campana" plaques.

Chiton

Tunic worn by the ancient Greeks, clinging to the body and held at the shoulder

by a clasp. Men wore the chiton either long or short, fastened only on the left or on both shoulders. Women wore chitons which came down to their toes.

Chiusi

One of the twelve powerful lucumonies of the Etruscan confederation, in northeastern Etruria. After Tarquinii the city richest in tombs (tombs of the Monkey, the Hill, Paolozzi fifth century B.C.). The tombs range over several centuries and enable us to follow the chronological development of Etruscan civilisation. The region produces an earth used for statues, bas-reliefs and canopic vases. The art of Chiusi presents features not found in other parts of Etruria.

157

Oenochoe
Corinthian style, late 7th century **B.C.**
Ibex, lioness and swan
Paris, Louvre

Choregos

Director of the theatre among the Greeks, responsible for controlling expenditure, whether the show was being put on at his own expense or that of the public. At Athens each of the ten tribes had its own choregos who vied in magnificence and taste with the others.

Clazomenai

Ancient city of Asia Minor on the south coast of the gulf of Smyrna. It enjoyed exceptional prosperity between the seventh and the middle of the sixth centuries B.C. Important centre for the manufacture of large terracotta sarcophagi decorated with paintings, also of vases exported to Ionia and Aeolia. The existing Turkish town of Urla stands on the site.

Colophon

City of Lydia (Asia Minor) north-west of Ephesus at the mouth of the Halesus, which claimed to be the birth-place of Homer.

Corinth

One of the most flourishing cities of ancient Greece. Situated at the end of the isthmus connecting the Peloponnese with the mainland, it was of great political and commercial importance. The city possessed two ports: Lechaea on the gulf of Corinth and Crencheae on the gulf of Aegina (Saronika) and could launch fleets both westward and eastward. Corinth was a great maritime power Enriched by this traffic, the city was filled with works of art. It was also a place of luxury and pleasure. Founded by the daughter of Phoroneus of Argos, Ephyra, it was governed by kings and later became an aristocratic republic which frequently allied with Sparta against Athens. It was captured and burnt by Mummius the Roman in 146 B.C. Traces of monuments ranging in date from archaic to Roman times have been discovered (temple of Apollo, agora, the famous Pirene fountain, etc.).

Cosmos

Greek word signifying order, harmony, beauty and also used of the world, the universal assemblage of all things. Pythagoras was the first to call the world the Cosmos, because of the proportion and harmony among all its component

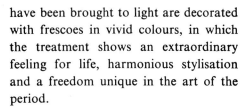

parts. All the Greek philosophers employ the word to designate the universe considered not as a mere heap of disconnected phenomena but as an ordered system wholly penetrated by finality.

Crete

Mediterranean island to the south-east of the Peloponnesos. Situated at the meeting-point of Europe, Africa and Asia, Crete was one of the most remarkable ancient centres of civilisation in the Mediterranean. Excavations have uncovered traces dating from an epoch of great antiquity which has been given the name Aegean or Minoan. The history of Crete occupies a place in the margin of that of continental Greece. One landmark is the arrival of invaders who came originally from Anatolia, about 2700 B.C. With them began the Bronze Age, which saw the island at its apogee. Unfortunately, the history of Crete is still very imperfectly known. In fact, despite the researches of Ventris which in 1953 made possible the deciphering of the most recent alphabet, the many other systems of writing still defy the efforts of the linguists. The walls of the palaces which

have been brought to light are decorated with frescoes in vivid colours, in which the treatment shows an extraordinary feeling for life, harmonious stylisation and a freedom unique in the art of the period.

Cumae

Greek city founded in Campania (Italy) by the Euboeans of Chalcis in the eleventh century B.C., well before the great movement in colonisation of Magna Graeca. Outside it was the shrine of a famous Sybil who is of interest because of the link established between her and the Sybilline Books at Rome.

Cyprus

Large island in the eastern Mediterranean. Phoenician territory, rich and fertile, it was colonised by the Greeks. The centre of the cult of Aphrodite, Cyprus possessed the most venerated sanctuaries in her honour: Paphos, Amathontos, Idalium, Golgos. In 58 B.C. Cyprus became part of the Roman Empire.

Cyrene

Greek city and colony established in Africa, west of Egypt. It was founded in 631 B.C. by Dorian colonists from Thera (Santorin) led by Battos, founder of the Battiades dynasty which long governed the city. Cyrene quickly became an important commercial city, almost equal with Carthage.

159

Gryphon, Palace of Darius I
Paris, Louvre

The Auriga (detail), about 475 B.C.
Museum at Delphi
Stamnos, third quarter of 5th century
Dionysiac festival (detail)
Paris, Louvre

D

Darius I

King of the Persians from 521-484 B.C.
He organised his empire, dividing it into
twenty satrapies, conquered India and
reduced Thrace and Macedon. He sent
an army to conquer Greece, but the
Greeks, under the guidance of Miltiades,
defeated him at Marathon (490 B.C.),
which put an end to the first Persian war.

Delos

The smallest of the Cyclades. From
earliest times it was a holy place. According to Greek legends it was here that
Apollo and Artemis were born. Delos
contained the great sanctuary dedicated
to Apollo and its celebrated oracle, also
the temples of Leto, Artemis, Hera, etc.
Until 454 B.C. the treasury of the Athenian
Confederation was on Delos. The island
still has an impressive group of ruins.
Numerous *objets d'art* have been found
there, notably some priceless mosaics.

160

Delphi

An important place in ancient Greece,
in Phocis, on a steep declivity on the
south-west slope of Mount Parnassus,
site of the sanctuary and oracle of Apollo.
The savage beauty of this spot, situated
in the middle of a huge enclosure of
bare rock, made it an ideal place for
heaving the revelations of Apollo from
the mouth of the Pythia, who had her
habitation in the Pytheum in the depths
of the temple. She would sit on a tripod
placed over a chasm in the rock, from
which vapours arose. She went into
trances and the priests interpreted her
utterances and movements.
The other buildings differ widely as to
date, style and importance. The principal
monuments include: the theatre, the
gymnasium, the famous Tholos or marble
rotunda. The sacred Castalia fountain is
at the exit of a gorge which divides the
Phaedriades rocks. Its waters ran through
the temple of Apollo. Delphi was loaded
with statues and precious objects in gold
and silver which have been pillaged on
several occasions: by the Phocidians
during the holy war, by the Gauls in

Stamnos, third quarter of 5th century
Dionysiac festival (detail)
Paris, Louvre

278 B.C., by the Thracians in 84, etc. The Pythian games were celebrated at Delphi every fourth year, in the spring. It was a meeting-place of the Amphictyonic Council.

Demetrius I Poliorcetes (the Besieger)

Son of Antigonos and king of Macedon (293-287 B.C.). He forced Cassander, protégé of Ptolemy, who had occupied the whole of Greece, to raise the siege of Athens and then defeated him near Thermopylae. He liberated the rest of Greece and in 303 revived the League of Corinth, being proclaimed its generalissimo. The Athenians instituted festivals in his honour.

Democritos

Greek philosopher born at Abdera in Thrace about 460 B.C., died about 370 B.C. Together with Leucippos, his master and friend, he was the creator of atomism. His theories, which are based on atomism, materialism and determinism, are remarkably close to those of modern science. He sees the universe as composed of emptiness and of indivisible and indestructible atoms, perpetually in motion and combining to form bodies of all kinds. Mind is itself composed of tenuous atoms. Democritus is considered one of the precursors of the atomic theory.

Diodorus Siculus

Greek historian, born at Agyrion in Sicily, living about the year 50 B.C. He spent thirty years in travel and investigations, in Europe, Asia, Egypt and at Rome, in order to collect the materials necessary for his *Bibliotheca Historica* (Historical Library), a work in forty volumes which covered the history of all the nations down to the time of Julius Caesar's conquest of Gaul. Considerable fragments of this work have come down to us; it is of particular interest for the summary it provides of a host of books now lost.

Dionysos, Festivals of

These festivals were introduced into Greece from Egypt, and because the archons presided at them, gave the year its name. The greater festivals had their mysteries (secret rites) and were celebrated in spring; the lesser festivals took place in autumn, at the time of the vintage. These ceremonies played an important part in the history of the theatre and of lyric poetry.

Dipylon

Ancient "double gateway" to Athens, the starting-point of the sacred way made

161

under the directions of Lycurgus (338-326), near which the remains of the famous Kerameikos necropolis have been discovered. The tombs contained huge funerary urns, some of them as much as 1.75 metres high, since known as the "Dipylon vases". A remarkable group of them can be seen in the National Museum of Athens.

Dithyrambs

Lyric poetry in honour of Dionysos, god of wine. One of the first poets to perfect the genre was Arion of Methymna (seventh century B.C.). The dithyramb was chanted by a choir performing evolutions round the altar of the god. The dithyramb is regarded as the earliest form of tragedy.

Douris

(First third of the fifth century B.C.) Painter, potter and decorator of the Attic school. His signature can be read on some thirty vases, the majority of them executed between 490 and 480. They are mostly decorated in red, though there are some in black. The style of Douris is severe, in his early works of a wholly archaic stiffness, for example, the cup showing Eos embracing the corpse of Memnon (Louvre). Later his manner becomes more supple and he acquires a truly Attic feeling for grace in the movement and elegance of his forms (*Interior of a school*, Berlin; *Ajax and Ulysses*, Vienna; *Amazons*, Brussels).

Ekphantos of Corinth

(Seventh century B.C.) Painter who came originally from Corinth. Contemporary with Kleanthes and Aedikides. According to Pliny, the first to break the monotony of monochrome by brightening the black with touches of red, derived from powdered brick. Painting might be said to begin with these high spots which enlivened the appearance of a picture.

Eleusis

Town in ancient Attica, 16 km. northwest of Athens, near the gulf of Aegina. It owed its fame to the mysteries celebrated there every five years (the Eleusinian mysteries) in honour of Demeter, Kore (Persephone) and Plonto. This trio of Chthonian deities shared a single mystery cult which was one of the most important in the Greek world. Preparation was by fasting, prayer and meditation; the initiates were called "epoptoi" or seers. Violation of the mysteries was punished by death. Eleusis apparently possessed from a very early date the sacred character it was to preserve throughout Antiquity.

Encaustic

Method of painting in use among the ancients, in which the colours were mixed with wax. Heated on the embers of a small stove, the coloured waxes were applied in liquid form with a brush. They were again reduced to this state when they had solidified in cooling on the picture. "Continuous application of heat was necessary. The 'cauterisers' or hot irons had to touch the colours, penetrate the wax, melt it and work it; they served to prolong the action of the brush, too brief for the purpose; they broke down the tones, making one merge into another, to produce modelling, to 'envelop', as it is termed" (Cros and Henry, "L'Encaustique"). Pliny ascribes the invention of encaustic painting to Aristeides of Thebes, who lived about 340 B.C. But, as he himself remarks, pictures of this type were known to have been executed by painters living long before Aristeides, for example, Polygnotos. It is impossible to verify this assertion, but we know from official records that this method was being used at Athens towards the end of the fifth century by the men who worked on the decoration to the cornice of the Erechtheion. It is likely that the use of this technique in Greece goes back to a much earlier period. It must have been introduced from Egypt in the seventh or sixth century.

Epaminondas

(420-362 B.C.) Famous Theban general and statesman. He expelled the Spartans from Thebes, defeated them at the battle of Leuctra (371 B.C.), four times invaded Laconia, relieved Messenia and was fatally wounded at Mantinea, defeating the Spartans. The greatness of Thebes died with him.

Ephesus

Ancient Ionian city, 60 km. south of Smyrna. Nothing remains of the temple of Artemis, built during the archaic period and considered one of the seven wonders of the world. It was burnt by Herostratus in 356. Another building, in whose decoration Skopas collaborated, was erected on the site, to be destroyed by Constantine. The buildings whose ruins can be seen today (Odeion, temples, libraries, theatre) were built by Lysimachus, one of Alexander's successors, in 287 B.C.

Epiktetos

Decorator of painted vases (third quarter of the sixth century) who worked at Athens. Links up with the miniaturist tradition inherited from Kleitias. His vases (of which twenty-seven are known) are interesting because the artist sometimes uses the archaic black-figured technique, sometimes red-figured decoration. His drawing is careful and graceful. He liked to depict ephebi ("Young horseman", British Museum; "Silenus", Cabinet des Mezdailles).

Epigram

Small piece of poetry on any subject in which the thought is pared down, satirical, expressed in a precise and biting fashion. Among the ancients, as the etymology of the word reveals ("epi", on and "graphe", I write), an epigram was originally a brief funerary or votive inscription scratched on a monument. It is, above all, from the Alexandrine era that it becomes an Independent poem with satirical intention.

Eretria

Ancient town on the west coast of the island of Euboea, commercial rival of Chalcis. It was destroyed by the Persians during the first Persian war (490 B.C.). Rebuilt, it retained some importance until the time of the Roman empire. From the end of the eighth century B.C. it was the site of numerous potters' workshops.

Ergotimos

Athenian potter of the first half of the sixth century B.C. Several pieces bearing his signature have survived, but he is best known as the author, with the painter Kleitias, of the famous "François vase" in the museum at Florence, one of the most remarkable examples of archaic black-figured pottery.

Eumaros

Painter of the archaic period. He must have lived towards the middle of the sixth century B.C. He was the father of Aulthenor, a celebrated sculptor. According to Pliny he was the first painter to distinguish female from masculine figures, by adopting for female flesh colouring found on vases of the antique style. Pliny adds that he was also the first "who

did not fear to present figures in all possible poses".

Eupatrides

Members of the hereditary nobility of ancient Attica. For a long time they had the monopoly of political rights. Their privileges were abolished by the Constitution of Solon, but they retained their priesthoods and also the great influence derived from their landed wealth. All citizens who were not eupatrides were classed either as "thetes", proletarians, or as "metics", foreigners.

Euphranor of Isthmia

Corinthian painter and sculptor of the fourth century B.C. He worked chiefly at Athens, where, according to Pausanias, he decorated the portico of Zeus Eleutherios at Kerameikos with pictures showing *The gods, Democracy, The People, Theseus, The charge of the Athenians at Mantinea*. His figures were distinguished for their elegance and slenderness. He was particularly skillful in rendering human emotions. He studied proportions and doubtless aimed at changing the canons of Polykleitas. As a sculptor of statues, he modelled gods or heroes mounted on quadrigae. He was the author of several treatises on symmetry and colours, but none of these works has come down to us.

Attic amphora by Exekias
About 530-520 B.C.
Return to Castor and Pollux (detail)
Ajax and Ulysses playing dice
Rome, Vatican Museum

Euphronios

Painter, and probably head of a work-shop, late sixth century B.C. His signature has been found on some fifteen vases, among them the earliest examples of red-figured decoration. Euphronios represents one of the peaks of Athenian painting on pottery and he had a great reputation among contemporaries. His "severe style" is remarkable for the purity of its drawing and the sobriety of its methods. Among his master-pieces one may mention the krater in the Louvre decorated with Herakles' struggle with Antaeos, the cup in the museum at Munich showing Herakles in combat with Geryon and another in the British Museum decorated with an Aphrodite.

Euripides

One of the three great tragic poets of Greece. Born at Salamis in 480 B.C., he was the son of a tavern-keeper and a vegetable seller. He studied painting, rhetoric, philosophy and was the friend of Socrates. He composed ninety-two tragedies, only nineteen of which are extant. His most highly regarded plays are "Medea", "The Phoenician Women", "Hippolytos" and "Iphigenia in Aulis". His work is remarkable for its psychological analysis of sexual passions. He endeavoured to rejuvenate the old myths and find new subjects. Towards the end of his life Euripides retired to the court of Archelaos, king of Macedon. He died there in 406, it is said eaten by dogs.

Euthymides

(Late sixth century B.C.) Painter, potter. He was preoccupied with the rendering of volume. Epiktetos was his disciple. He is one of the best representatives of the "severe style". See his amphora decorated with "Antiope and her companions" in the museum at Munich, where he loosens the conventional types and suggests, with much that is natural, the movement of the bodies.

Exekias

One of the greatest of the black-figure Attic school of painter potters. He worked towards the middle of the sixth century B.C. Author of a monumental amphora "Ajax and Achilles playing dice" (Vatican Museum) and of the Munich cup illustrating the "Voyages of Dionysos". The vases painted by this artist are not very numerous, but his influence was considerable. His act aims at the monumental, while remaining within the framework of a severe archaism.

165

Attic krater, the "François vase"
About 475 B.C.
Signed by Kleitias and Ergotimos (detail)
Hunting scene
Florence, Archaeological Museum

Falerii

One of the twelve cities of ancient Etruria, in the southern part of the region, not far from the Tiber. In 395 B.C. it surrendered to Camillus, who was besieging it. Falerii revolted against Rome on several occasions and was destroyed in 241. The city was the capital of the Faliscans. Among the ruins are those of an Etruscan temple from the fourth century B.C.

Fikellura

Ancient necropolis on the island of Rhodes, close to Camiros.

Frieze

Name given to a flat, continuous horizontal surface, whose length far exceeds its height, adorned with paintings or sculptures.

Gla

Islet in what was once Lake Copais (Boeotia), which has now dried up. It harboured a royal residence built towards the fifteenth century B.C. whose ruins recall those of Mycenae. The plan of the palace is reminiscent of certain parts of the labyrinth on Crete with its two sets of boxes placed at right angles.

Glaukos of Chios

Greek statue maker of the early sixth century B.C. Disciple of Agheledas. The ancients alleged that he invented the tempering of iron and soldering. He was the author of a silver krater with an iron base which was offered to the temple of Delphi by Alyattes, king of Lydia. Atheneus and Pausanias, who describe this base, very famous in Antiquity, say it was decorated in relief with small animals and plants. According to one tradition, Glaukos also discovered the square, the lever and the lathe.

Gnatia

Place close to Tarentum where vases in a particular style were made, in which black glaze plays a principal role. It invaded the entire vase; white ornaments, highlighted with vivid yellow and red are the only alleviation to the sombre hue of the ground. (Second half of the third century B.C.)

Hydria by Meidias
5th century B.C.
Amorous scene
Florence, National Museum of Antiquities

Gournia

Place near Heraklion in eastern Crete. American excavations carried out 1901-1904 uncovered an ancient town from the beginning of the Late Minoan Age.

Gynaeieum

In a Greek house, the part inhabited by the women. Greek women led a secluded life and their apartment was a sanctuary forbidden to all strangers and open only to husbands, a little like the harems of the East. The surveillance of the gynaeceum fell in particular to the porters, who were often eunuchs. In the middle of the apartments was a large salon ("oikos"), where the mistress of the house passed her time, usually in spinning or weaving. On one side of it was the bed-chamber ("thalamos"), on the other a room reserved for the attendant slaves ("amphithalamoi").

Hagia Triada

Place 60 km. from Heraklion in Crete where excavations have brought to light a large palace, probably belonging to a lord who was vassal of the princess of Phaistos, a necropolis and a village dating from 1900 to 1400 B.C. The discoveries include frescoes, decorated soapstone vases (the "Harvesters" among them) and a remarkable painted sarco-phagus.

Helena of Alexandria

Daughter of the painter Timon, to whom is ascribed a *Battle of Alexander with Darius at Issus*. She belongs to the "Asiatic" school and must have lived towards the end of the fourth century.

Herodotos

(484-424 B.C.) "The Father of History." Born at Halicarnassos (Asia Minor). To escape from the tyranny of Lygdamis, he took refuge at Samos and later made long journeys in Europe, Asia and Africa, everywhere he went taking careful note of the history, traditions, laws, customs and learning of the people he was visiting. On his return from his many voyages he seems to have spent some time at Athens and was one of the party of colonists sent to Thurii in Magna Graeca in 444 B.C. Here he passed the rest of his life. In the first four of the nine books of his

167

"History", he introduces the different peoples who took part in the great Greco-Persian struggle, a struggle recounted in the remaining five books.

Hesiod

One of the earliest Greek poets, born probably towards the middle of the seventh century B.C. at Askra (Boeotia), where his father, a native of Kyme in Aeolis, had settled. Three poems under the name of Hesiod have come down to us. The first, "Works and Days", is a collection of exhortations, moral, political and economic. In addition there is the "Theogony", in which the poet relates the birth of the universe and the genealogy of the gods, and the "Shield of Herakles" an account of Herakles' fight with Kyknos.

Hieron

Hieron I.—Tyrant of Gela and Syracuse, successor to his brother Gelon. He reigned from 478-467 B.C. He made Syracuse glorious by its arms and flourishing by its arts. His victories at Olympia and Delphi were sung by Pindar, who visited him, as did Aeschylos.
Hieron II.—King of Syracuse, born towards 306, died about 216 B.C. He distinguished himself under Pyrrhus and later against the Mamertini. Elected king by the people in 270 he at first sought the alliance of the Carthaginians, but soon abandoned them in favour of the Romans. His gentleness, wise laws and thrift—which did not prevent him from

generous aid to his allies in their distress —and the encouragement he gave to the researches of Archimedes all helped to make his memory dear to the Syracusans.

Hipparchos

Son of Peisistratos whom he succeeded, jointly with his brother Hippias, in 527 B.C. They governed wisely and were patrons of arts and letters. It is said that Hipparchos brought the Homeric poems to Athens; he summoned to his side Anacreon and Simonides and created a library. But he violated the sister of a young Athenian named Harmodios and in 514 died victim to a conspiracy he formed with his friend Aristogeiton.

Hippias

Son of Peisistratos, whom he succeeded, jointly with his brother Hipparchos, in 527 B.C. The cruelties he perpetrated after the assassination of his brother brought about his banishment from Athens in 510. Taking refuge with Darius, he incited him to invade Attica and marched with the Persian army against his homeland, to perish among their ranks at Marathon, in 490.

Horace

In Latin, Quintus Horatius Flaccus. Latin poet born at Venusia (Apulia) in 65, died at Rome in 8 B.C. Son of a freedman, he received at Rome the education given to the sons of the best families and then went on to study philosophy at Athens. Briefly enrolled in the army of Brutus, Caesar's murderer, he hastened to profit from the amnesty following the battle of Philippi to return to Rome, where he found that part of his father's patrimony had been confiscated. But his earliest verse (satires and odes) soon made him known to Virgil and Varius, who introduced him to Maecenas; the latter became his friend and in turn introduced him to Augustus. Benefactions from these two made it possible for Horace, whose tastes were modest, to achieve that "golden mediocrity" which satisfied his ambition. He passed the greater part of his life either in his house on the Tiber or on a small Sabine estate, composing at his leisure the charming poetry which has immortalised his name, to wit: four books of odes, one of epodes, two of satires and two of epistles, of which the last, the epistle to Piso usually goes under the name of the "Poetic Art".

Hypogea

(Greek "hupo", under, and "ge", ground) —name given by the Ancients to the subterranean constructions in which they deposited their dead. Hypogea occur in large numbers in all the countries of the Mediterranean littoral. They are generally decorated with fresco paintings, mosaics, figures in relief, etc.

I

Iktinos

(Fifth century B.C.) One of the most famous architects of Greece. Nothing is known of his life. His most celebrated work is the Parthenon on the acropolis at Athens, He collaborated with Kallikrates, and with a certain Karpion wrote a book, now lost, describing the temple. In this monument he applied the rules of the Doric order in all their rigour. Iktinos was also responsible for the hall of initiation known as the "secos mystikos" at Eleusis. It is possible that he assisted Pheidias in the modifications to the cella of the temple of Zeus at Olympia. He also drew the plans for the temple of Apollo Epikourios at Bassae, near Phygalia in Arcadia, in which he was able to mingle the Ionic and the Doric in harmonious fashion.

Ionia

Ancient region on the coast of Asia Minor, contained between the rivers Hermes and Maeander. It took this name after the immigration of the Ionians in 1140 B.C., led by the sons of Kodros. They founded twelve cities, the chief of them being Ephesus, Phocaea, Chios, Samos, Colophon and Miletus, which formed a confederation. Letters, the sciences and the arts were being cultivated in Ionia from an early date. Fatherland of Homer, Anacreon, Anaxagoras, Pythagoras, Thales of Miletus, Heraclitos, Aspasia, etc. From the time of Croesus, sixth century B.C., the

Ionian hydria, "Caeretan" (detail)
540-520 B.C.
Herakles. Paris, Louvre

Ionians lost their independence and had to submit to the rule of all the conquerors of Asia Minor down to the Romans, who occupied Ionia in 133 B.C.

Issos

Ancient city of Asia Minor in Cilicia, on the sea at the base of the gulf of Issika. It is memorable for the three victories secured in its neighbourhood, one by Alexander over Darius in 333 B.C., the second by Septimius Severus over Pescennius Niger in A.D. 194 and the third by Heraclius over Chosroes in 622.

Kallimachos

Sculptor and engraver of the second half of the fifth century B.C. Pliny mentions his *Lacedaemoneans dancing* and also his statue *Seated Hera*, showing her as the bride of Zeus, executed for the Heraion at Plataea. His manner was characterised by meticulous attention to detail, hence his sonbriquet, "Catalexitechnos". According to a story told by Vitruvius he was the inventor of the Corinthian capital. The idea came to him while he was looking at a flowering acanthus wreathed round a basket placed on a child's tomb.

Kalliphon of Samos

(Second half of the seventh century B.C.) Pausanias, who alone mentions this artist, says he composed a picture showing women adjusting the plates of Patroklos' cuirass. He had also painted in the temple of Artemis at Ephesus a *Battle of the Greeks and Trojans* taking place in the vicinity of Patroklos' fleet, one of the episodes in the Iliad.

Kamares

Cave on the southern slope of Mount Ida in Crete, at a height of 1520 m. English archaeologists found there a considerable number of vases in a particular style, now known as the Kamares style.

650 B.C. Its necropoleis have yielded a large number of late Attic vases. The presence of Kertch vases has also been noted in the region of Naples, in Gallo-Greek necropoleis in southern France and in Catalonia. The favourite shapes are the bell krater and the pelike. The Kertch style continued down to the last quarter of the fourth century.

Kamiros

One of the three ancient towns which united towards the end of the fifth century B.C. to form the city of Rhodes. Excavations of the Italian school have uncovered an entire town with temples and houses on the site.

Kerameikos

Quarter of Athens to the north-west of the city which from the time of the Peisistratids contained the agora. Its name is probably derived from the potters' workshops situated there. It was also the site of the large ancient cemetery which contained the most famous tombs, in particular those raised by the republic in honour of those who had died for their country. The presence of a necropolis in this district dates from the twelfth century B.C. The oldest portion of it has yielded the "Dipylon" vases.

Kertch

Town in the Crimaea, in Antiquity Pantikapaea, colonised by Miletus about

Kimon of Kelonai

Painter from the end of the sixth century B.C., who was the dominant figure of his day. He seems to have been the precursor of the great painters of the fifth century; it is accepted that he invented figures seen as "foreshortened". According to Pliny, Kimon also marked much more clearly than his predecessors the attachments of limbs and the ridge made by veins in the flesh. He was no less successful in rendering the softness of materials, the shadow lines and the sinuous curves traced by folds on the surface of draperies.

Kleathes of Corinth

(Seventh century B.C.) He is considered one of the precursors of classical painting because of the perfection in his rendering of the human silhouette. Strabo mentions two works of his placed close to the temple at Olympia, one representing the sack of Troy, the other the birth of Athena. This is all that is known for certain about this artist of the archaic period.

171

Kleophrades

Athenian painter of the beginning of the fifth century B.C. He is identified with the painter Epiktetos.

Kleitias

Athenian painter potter of the first half of the sixth century B.C. He painted the "François vase" potted by Ergotimos. This vase, one of the most important in the Greek pottery of the sixth century, was found near Chiusi in 1844 and is called after its discoverer. The "François vase" is a first essay in what was to become the "krater". The painter has introduced nearly two hundred carefully observed figures, arranged in super-imposed zones. The subjects include: the return of Theseus after his victory over the Minotaur, the hunt for the Kalydon boar, the chariot races at the funeral of Patroclus, Archilles in pursuit of Troilus and Polyxena, etc.

Knossos

The largest Minoan site discovered in Crete. Its royal palace, houses, traces of flagged roadways and its aqueduct make it one of the most important documents of Antiquity. Knossos reached its apogee towards 1500 B.C. under the legendary king Minos. It was twice destroyed, once about 1400 B.C. and again towards the end of the eleventh century B.C. Starting in the late nineteenth century, the excavations of Sir Arthur Evans and his successors have unearthed and restored the palace and its adjacent tombs. These have yielded an extraordinary harvest of *objects d'art*, frescoes, coloured faience ware, painted terrocotta vases, etc. See "Crete".

Kraton of Sikyon

Painter of the late seventh century B.C. Contemporary with Kleanthes. Known only from a mention in the writings of Athenagoras who ascribes to him the invention of monochrome painting: he was the first, he says, to paint silhouettes of men and women on a panel covered with white colouring.

Kypselos

Tyrant of Corinth. He dedicated at Olympia a casket, whose author is unknown, which was ornamented with a scene from the Argonaut cycle. It is described at length by Pausanias.

Latium

Territory of ancient Italy situated along the length of the Tyrrhenian sea, between Etruria and Campania. A distinction was made as follows: 1. The old Latium, or Latium properly speaking, to the north. Principal towns: Alba, Praeneste, Pedum, Tibur, Algidum, Fregella, etc., which formed a confederation (the Hernici and Rome were classed geographically with old Latium although they did not form part of it); 2. The new Latium, to the south; principal tribes: the Aequi, the Volsci, the Rutuli, the Ausonii or Auruncii; towns: Anagnia, Suessa Pometia, Velitrae, Antium, Auximum, Ardea, Suessa Arunca. This latter region was not really part of Latium and was not integrated with it until the time of the Roman conquest. The subjugation of Latium by the Romans started in the time of Romulus. In 664 the Romans forced Alba to submit. Under Tarquinius Superbus the Confederation of Latium (with the exception of Gabii) in 498 recognised the supremacy of Rome; Gabii was taken in 496. The Aequi and the Volsci submitted in 367, revolted in 345 and again in 338 but were finally crushed in 314. The Romans covered Latium with colonies and municipia.

Leagros

Strategos, colleague of Themistocles. He died in Thrace in 465. The last decade of the sixth century has been given the name "age of Leagros" inscriptions referring to Leagros (a fairly uncommon name) are found on the vases of this period.

Lesche

Places of meeting and for gossip. The lesche was the building in which the citizens of a Greek city met to converse—they would correspond to our clubs. There were many throughout Greece, probably one in each town. The most famous is that of Delphi, which served as a meeting-place for everyone—Greeks and foreigners—attracted to Delphi by the oracle and the Pythian Games. There was also a very fine lesche at Sparta.

Lucian

One of the wittiest of Greek writers. Born at Samosata in Syria about 125, died in Egypt about A.D. 192. He excelled in sophistical elegance and toured Asia Minor, Greece, Italy and Gaul, giving lectures prepared in advance. He then embarked on a relentless war against the prejudices and vices of his time; his lively and biting satires are comic portraits, full of life and truth, of the moral and religious condition of second century society. His "Dialogues of the gods", "Sailors' dialogues", "Dialogues of courtesans" and above all "Dialogues of the dead" are the best known works of this Voltaire of Antiquity. Lucian attacks the philosophers of all schools, or rather holds up to ridicule imposters who usurp the name of philosopher. He is the enemy of superstition and in his capacity of sceptical philosopher hits out at new and old cults indiscriminately. His style has a sustained elegance, a piquant Atticism.

Lucumonies

Name given to the federation of twelve Etruscan towns. Despite their ethnic unity, the Etruscans never came together to form a state. Each town of the federation had its own laws under an oligarchichal constitution which entrusted supreme authority to the magistrates, known as lucumons.

Lydia

Ancient territory of Asia Minor lying between Phrygia on the east and the Greek colonies on the west. Towns: Sardis, the capital, Apollonia, Larissa, Magnesia of Sipyle, Metropolis, etc. Inhabited initially by the Pelasgi, Lydia later knew three successive dynasties of kings: the Alyades, the Heraklides and the Mermnades. Under Croesus the kingdom of Lydia embraced the whole of Asia Minor west of the Halys. Cyrus destroyed it at a single blow at the battle of Thymbra, 548. From then on Lydia was subjected to the Persians, the Macedonians, the kings of Syria and of Pergamon. It was eventually ceded to Rome, under the will of king Attalus III of Pergamon, in 129 B.C.

Lydos

Painter. Worked during the second half of the sixth century B.C. His name is probably a soubriquet meaning that he was a "Lydian", who had fled to Athens because of the Persian invasions.

Macedonia

State of ancient Europe, in north-eastern Greece. In Greek tradition, Macedonia owed its name to the "Macedues", a Pelasgian tribe established in Emathia in the fourteenth century B.C. The true founder of the kingdom, however, seems to have been the Heraklid Caranas who came from Argos, which gave him Edessa as his capital in 799. Under the successors of this prince Macedonia expanded and under Alexander I started to play a part in the Persian war; it was powerful under Philip II, who prepared the ruin of the Persian empire, accomplished by Alexander III the Great between 336 and 323. His death delivered Macedonia over to fifty years of countless usurpations until the day when Antigonos Gonatas was left master of the throne, in 273. Shortly afterwards Macedonia came under the threat of Roman domination: defeated under Philip III at Cynosoephalae in 197, crushed at Pydna in 168

during the reign of Perses, Macedonia was finally reduced to a province in 148, after the revolt of Andriscos.

Makron

Painter of red-figured vases (early fifth century B.C.). Collaborated with the potter Hieron on the skyphos found at Suessula, which presents the "Story of Helen". He belongs to the last phase of the "severe style". His work is highly original. He has a very sensuous manner of rendering the human form, male as well as female. The clothing and headdresses of his women have a provocative elegance; their bodies show freely beneath transparent draperies.

Mallia

Place 34 km. from Heraklion (Crete). Excavation has revealed a large palace contemporary with the first palaces of Knossos and Phaistos, dating from Middle Minoan I.

Mandrokles of Samos

Herodotos relates that Mandrokles, the architect responsible for building the bridge of boats thrown across the Bosporos during Darius' expedition to 506, made a painting to commemorate the event. The great king was shown seated on his throne on the shore, presiding over the march past of the army as it crossed the strait. Later on Mandrokles dedicated this painting to the Heraion at

Samos. This evidence, taken in conjunction with what Pliny says of Boularchos, suggests that portable pictures were known in Ionià from an early date.

Marathon

One of the most ancient demes of Attica, 30 km. north-east of Athens. According to mythology, Theseus overcame a bull which was devastating the surrounding plain. Marathon is famous for the battle fought there by Miltiades against the Persians in 490 B.C., which brought the first Persian war to an end. The Athenians won the day and disclosed their full strength.

Meidias

Potter of the Attic school who worked at the end of the fifth century B.C. The works attributed to him are in the "florid" style, insisting on details of decoration and drapery, which are highlighted in gold and white. His elegance is somewhat affected. (Hydria with the "Rape of the Leucippides" and "Herakles in the garden of the Hesperides", British Museum.)

Melanthios

Painter of the four century B.C. Pupil of Pamphilos. Lived at Sikyon. Head of a school and author of a book on painting used by Pliny, a fragment of which has been preserved by Diogenes Laertius. None of his works is known. The Ancients agreed that he had a great talent for composition, surpassing in this all his colleagues in the same studio and all his rivals, even Apelles (Pliny xxxv, 80). Several pictures by Melanthios were in the possession of Aratus and passed later to the Ptrolemies. The most famous of them is described by Plutarch. It showed Aristatos of Sikyon standing beside the chariot of Victory.

Melos

176

Ancient name for the island of Milo, one of the southern Cyclades. Colonised first by the Phoenicians and later by the Spartans, the island was conquered in 417 B.C. by the Athenians who sacked it and massacred the inhabitants. Extant are the ruins of a temple and also of a magnificent marble amphitheatre, among which a peasant found in 1820 the celebrated statue known as the Venus de Milo, broken into several pieces and buried under the rubble.

Metope

Square space which in the frieze to the entablature of a Doric building alternates with the triglyphs (ornamental salbs usually with three vertical channels). The metopes are most frequently decorated with sculpted reliefs. The metopes of the Parthenon are famous. Pheidias left their execution to his pupils. In vase painting a "metope arrangement" is one in which the decoration consists of surrounding a colourless zone, reserved for figures, with a black colour spread over the greater part of the belly.

Mikon

Painter and statue maker, early fifth century B.C. He was a pupil of Polygnotos and with him laid the foundations for the representation of space. In collaboration with his master, he decorated the portico known as the Poikile in the agora at Athens. To the left of the

Ilioupersis, a major composition by Polygnotos, he executed, with assistance from Pheidias' brother Panainos, a *Battle of Marathon*. The defeated Barbarians were shown in precipitate retreat, some taking to the swamps, others to their boats. On the other side of the *Ilioupersis* Mikon recounted Theseus' battle with the Amazons. After Mikon's time Amazon battles increase in popularity, both in sculpture and in vase painting. He was also responsible for pictures in the sanctuary of Theseus at Athens, a *Battle of the Centaurs and Lapiths*, a *Visit of Theseus to Amphitrite and Poseidon* and a *Death of Theseus*. He painted a *Departure of the Argonauts* in the Anakeion. As sculptor, Mikon executed the statue of the "Athenian Kallias", Olympic victor. In place of allegory and allusion, Mikon introduced veracity and historical exactitude, thus following a trend also making itself manifest in the literature of his time. His daughter Timarete, author of an *Artemis*, is regarded as the first woman painter.

Miletus

Ancient Ionian city on the west coast of Asia Minor, south of the mouth of the Maeander. In the time of its greatness, the eighth to sixth centuries B.C., Miletus is said to have had up to three hundred colonies on the Black Sea or Propontis. After Tyre it was the biggest trading city in the world. It engaged in all the traffic of the North, in corn, dried fish, slaves and skins. Fatherland of

Thales, Anaximander, Aspasia, Aeschines, Aristides, etc. Miletus was the seat of the Ionian school of philosophy.

Mnesikles

Athenian architect of the second half of the fifth century, who built the Propylaea on the Acropolis at Athens, between 437 and 432 B.C. The Peloponnesian war prevented the work from being finished. Mnesikles knew how to make a skilful blend of the Doric and Ionic orders and contrasts in masterly fashion the grey-blue limestone of Eleusis with the white marble of Pentelicus.

Mycenae

One of the chief cities of the Argolis, north-east of Argos, close to Mount Tretos. Some claim that its founder was Mycene, daughter of Inachos (about 1480), others that it was Acrisios or Perseus. It was the principal city of Greece during the era of the Mycenaean civilisation (from 1400). Capital of a small kingdom, Mycenae disputed with Argos for supremacy over the Peloponnese. The kings belonged to the celebrated dynasty of the Atrides (Agamemnon, Clytemnestra, Aegisthos, Orestes, etc.), who had a palace and a necropolis made for themselves. Mycenae was ruined by the Dorian invasion, to the benefit of Argos. It nevertheless survived as a small independent city and took part in the Persian wars. The Argives, allied with the inhabitants of Kleonai and

Tegea, destroyed it totally in 470 B.C. The remains of its monuments, which have endured for three thousand years, rank among the architectural and archaeological marvels of the world: the Lion Gate, the Treasury of Atreus, the Cyclopean walls. Golden ornaments discovered in the tombs are of capital importance for archaeology and testify to the wealth and strength of the Mycenaean kings. Mycenae has given its name to the art which dominates the Late Bronze Age, whose influence was felt in Greece and the Eastern Mediterranean.

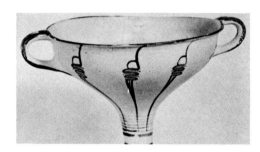

Naukratis

Ancient Greek city in Egypt, situated on the Nile delta. Founded from Miletus in the seventh century B.C. In the sixth century the pharaoh Ahmes decreed it should be the sole port open to the Greeks and all Greek merchants in Egypt were obliged to settle there. From that time it played a very important part in trade between Egypt and the Greek world. Naukratis was famed for its vases, its flowers and its courtesans. The rise of Alexandria brought about its decline.

Nearchos

Painter potter of the second quarter of the sixth century B.C. Author of black-figured vases. Contemporary with Kleitias and Ergotimos and like them a worker in the miniaturist style. In a vase fragment representing Achilles preparing for battle, he marries the perfection of the detail to a grandeur and simplicity of form.

Necropolis

(From the Greek "nekros", dead, and "polis", city.) The portion of ancient cities corresponding to our cemeteries. From the architectonic point of view it applies primarily to a group of burials presenting a monumental character.

Nikias of Athens

Athenian painter (middle of the fourth century B.C.). Attached to the school of Euphranor. He was the son of Nikomachos. He collaborated with Praxiteles in the polychromy of his statues. It is said that he had such a passion for his art that he neglected to eat and drink. Nikias was a considerable painter, judging from the many references to him in ancient writings and the number of works they attribute to him. Pliny says that he "painted women with meticulous care". His celebrated *Io* and *Andromeda* are known to us from replicas made by the frescoists of Pompeii and Rome. He also painted battles, naval engagements, an *Evocation of the Dead* after the *Odyssey*, a *Portrait of Alexander*, etc. Nikias doubtless also worked in encaustic. He excelled in rendering the contrasts of light and shade and was the first to use cinnabar for shading.

Nirou Chani

Place 13 km. from Heraklion, Crete, where a building dating from Late Minoan I (about 1550-1450 B.C.) has been discovered; according to A. Evans it was the residence of a chief priest. Important centre for the manufacture of cult objects.

Temple of Zeus, west pediment
Centaur biting the arm of a Lapith
Museum at Olympia

Olympus

Range of Greek mountains between Macedon and Thessaly. The Greeks identified one of its peaks, 2,985 m. high, as the dwelling of the gods.

Olympia

Religious centre of the Peloponnesos (Elis), where the famous Olympic Games celebrated in honour of Olympian Zeus were held. Situated at the foot of Mount Kronion, it was not properly speaking a town. It was a vast sanctuary, the most important of those dedicated to Zeus, where every four years the great Pan-Hellenic festivals were held. The valley in which it was situated was famed for its tranquillity and for its balmy air. This soothing atmosphere was favourable to reconciliations between the warring brothers of the Pan-Hellenic race. A fantastic number of works of art decorated the superb temple of Zeus, as also the sacred wood surrounding it. The active life of Olympia lasted more than ten centuries, until A.D. 393, date of the last Olympic Games to be held in Antiquity. The most ancient building extant is the temple of Hera. The *Hermes* of Praxiteles was unearthed here. On the temple of Zeus, metopes have been found representing the twelve labours of Herakles, and also pediments (chariot race of Pelops and Oenomaos, fight Lapiths and the Centaurs) which rank among the most beautiful works of pre-Classical sculpture. Nothing has survived of the chryselephantine (i.e. gold and ivory) statue of Zeus, Pheidias' masterpiece.

Orchomenos

City of Boeotia, one of the oldest and richest cities of heroic Greece. Capital of the legendary Minyans. Its treasures are boasted in the *Iliad*. A very prosperous commercial centre between from the eighth to the sixth centuries, it was progressively undermined by Thebes, who subdued and sacked it in 364 B.C. Restored by Philip of Macedon, it was again ruined at the beginning of the Christian era. It was the centre of a brilliant civilisation. The Charites or Graces were venerated here and festivals held in their honour; the cult of Asklepios was also fostered. This city has also been identified as the site of the Oracle of Tiresias and the tomb of Hesiod.

Orvieto

Italian town in the province of Perugia.

Pagasae

Ancient town of Thessaly, situated north of the gulf from which it takes its name. It was the port of Iolkos, capital of Mycenaean Thessaly. According to the legend, it was here that Jason, leader of the Argonauts, built the ship "Argo" on which he embarked for Colchis. The town had a famous oracle. A large quantity of funerary stelae in polychrome stone have been found embedded in the walls, precious testimony to very early painting.

Palaestra

Public place for training in various bodily exercises and games which developed both dexterity and physical strength. Most of these establishments had porticoes, hot and cold baths and even rooms for lessons in grammar and philosophy. The exercises and games, sometimes given the name palaestra, included running, jumping, wrestling, boxing, discus, throwing, etc.

Pamphilos of Amphipolis

Greek painter (fourth century B.C.). Pupil of Eupompos of Sikyon who was the founder of an important local school. The ancient authors present Pamphilos as a learned theoretician who insisted on the great profit painting could derive from arithmetic, geometry and all the sciences. He was the first to introduce drawing into the curriculum of the Sikyon schools, an example soon followed all over Greece. Among his works mention is made of a *Fight between the Heraklides and the Athenians* and *Ulysses on his ship.* He had numerous pupils, including Pausias of Sikyon, Melanthios and the grand Apelles of Cos.

Panainos

Greek painter, second quarter of the fifth century B.C. Native of Athens, brother or nephew of Pheidias, with whom he collaborated. Pheidias entrusted him with the painted decoration to the throne of the gold and ivory statue of Zeus, executed by the Sculptor for the temple at Olympia. Between the columns of the throne Panainos represented: *Herakles and Atlas, Herakles and the Nemean lion, The Garden of the Hesperides, Theseus and Pirithous, Hippodamia, Prometheus, The death of Panthesilea, Ajax violating Cassandra* and two allegorical figures, *Hellas* and *Salamis.* He painted several other frescoes in the same temple, but the subjects are not reported by the ancient authors. At Elis, the paintings on the shield of the statue of Athena, the work of Kolotes, a disciple of Pheidias, were attributed to Panainos. He finished the *Battle of Marathon* in the Stoa Poikile at Athens, begun by Mikon.

Panathenian Festivals

Celebrated at Athens in honour of the goddess Athena, patron of the city. According to legend founded by Theseus.

Parrhasios

Ephesian painter who lived at Athens during the second half of the fifth century B.C. Son and pupil of Evenor, with Zeuxis he is the most illustrious of the Ionian school. As against the decorative and monumental painting of Polygnotos, they favour the easel picture, develop the pictorial effect proper by means of exact observation of the proportions, plastic relief, the play of lights and shades, the facial expressions. Their knowledge of drawing and colour was sufficient to allow them to indulge in *trompe-l'oeuil*. Among the many anecdotes on the subject the following, told by Pliny, may be cited: Zeuxis had painted a bunch of grapes so life-like that the birds came to peck at them, whereupon Parrhasios painted on top a linen curtain, so convincing that Zeuxis asked him to pull it aside. The Ancients have preserved for us the name of numerous works by Parrhasios: *Agamemnon and Ulysses, Herakles and Perseus, Dionysos and Virtue, Ulysses feigning madness*, and some erotic scenes, *Atlanta and Meleager* and the *Archigallus*, bought by Tiberius; finally he was the author of a famous picture of the Athenian *Demos* which he succeeded in representing under its most contradictory aspects: inconstant, irascible, unjust, frivolous, docile, cautious, compassionate, generous, proud, mean, brave, indolent.

Pausanias

Second century A.D. Historian, geographer, mythologist and historian of Greek art. Author of an important work entitled *Itinerary of Greece*. It is a king of guide-book, covering the Peloponnesos, Attica, Boeotia, and Phocis, together with a brief mention of the adjacent islands and some cities on the Asiatic shore. This document is of capital importance for archaeology and the history of the fine arts, because it describes, with great precision, monuments, paintings, sculptures and statues which no longer exist and are known to us only from this account, in particular the paintings in the Poikile at Athens and those of Polygnotos at Delphi, the "Olympian Jupiter" of Pheidias and all the master-pieces surrounding it, etc.

Pausias of Sikyon

Greek painter of the Sikyon school (fourth century B.C.). Pupil of his father, Bryes, and of Pamphilos. Primarily a decorator. According to Pliny he was the first to paint ceilings. He mingled his garlands, scrolls and interlace with little genre subjects, showing a special fondness for children. He was the inventor of this genre which was much cultivated during the Alexandrine period and of which the houses at Pompeii give an excellent idea. Pausias had as his mistress Glycera, who composed floral bouquets and wreathes. He too took to painting flowers, and became very skilful in the rendering of bouquets. He is cited as the author of a *Sacrifice of Oxen*, in which one of the beasts was viewed from the front and foreshortened. Furthermore, this ox was painted in a single black colour, the reflections giving the sole indication of the modelling. Pausias has also been credited with discovering how to render glass transparent. He painted at Epidauros a picture of Drunkennes, whose countenance was viewed through a glass.

Peisistratos

Tyrant of Athens, born about 612 B.C. Related to Solon. He wooed the crowd to win supreme personal power, had himself voted a bodyguard by the people, seized the citadel and established himself there openly as a tyrant (560). In 554 he was expelled by the supporters of Lykourgos and Megakles, but the latter then helped him back into power. From 554 he was again out of power for eleven years but was restored and handed his authority on to his sons Hipparchos and Hippias. He embellished Athens, built a temple to Olympian Jupiter and had the Homeric rhapsodies collected and published. He died in 527.

Pella

Ancient town of Macedonia, 39 km. from Salonika, from the end of the fifth century B.C. the capital of the Macedonian kings. Philip and Alexander the Great were born there. Excavations by Greek archaeologists under official auspices have been in progress there since 1957. Notable discoveries include mosaic pavements composed from polychrome pebbles (Hellenistic period), which show the following subjects: a pair of Centaurs, a gryphon devouring a stag, three compositions with Dionysos seated on a panther, hunting scenes.

Peloponnesos

Southerly peninsula of Greece, attached to the mainland by the isthmus of Corinth and comprising the Argolis, Corinthia, Laconia, Messenia, Elis, Achaia, Arcadia. Notable events in its history include: the foundation of the kingdom of Argos by Inachos about 1986, of Sikyon about 1920, of Sparta about 1880, of Corinth about 1350; the arrival of Pelops of Phrygia, who reigned in Elis about 1350 and gave his name to the whole peninsula; the expulsion of the Heraklides about 1300, their various attempts to return to the Peloponnesos, finally achieved with Dorian assistance (1190); the occupation of the principal thrones of the territory by various members of this dynasty; the Messenian wars (743 and 685); the establishment of Spartan ascendancy in the Peloponnesos, their rivalry with the Athenians, which gave rise to the Peloponnesian war (431-404) and led to the domination of Sparta; the wars between Sparta and Thebes (371-363), during which the Peloponnese was several times invaded; the efforts

183

of the Achaean league to repulse the Romans, the struggle of this league against Sparta, and finally the reduction of the Peloponnesos, together with the rest of Greece, to a Roman province under the name of Achaia.

Pergamon

Ancient city of Asia Minor, founded in 282 B.C. Famous for the invention of parchment. Its library, founded by Eumenes II, had 200,000 volumes and was second only to that of Alexandria (Mark Antony had to make a present of it to Cleopatra). Attalus I and his successors embellished the city with sumptuous buildings, among them the monumental "Great Altar" set up in 180, dedicated to Zeus and Athena Nike. It was ornamented with a sculpted frieze 120 m. long, representing the "Battles of Gods and Giants" (now in the Archaeological Museum of East Berlin).

Pericles

Athenian statesman (493-429 B.C.). Whilst still very young won fame and popularity by his eloquence and liberality. About 459 became head of the democratic party, in opposition to Kimon. Banished for a time (457) but ended as master of the situation (444). His administration stands out for the construction of magnificent buildings, for example the Parthenon and the Propylaea, lavish festivals, the distribution of bounties to the poor citizens of Athens and great external successes. His policy was to shun far-

flung and hazardous enterprises, and to consolidate the power of Athens and her superiority over Sparta. Even so, he was unable to avert a breach between the two republics, which gave rise to the Peloponnesian war. He was even accused of provoking the war, by supporting the Corcyreans in their revolt against their metropolis, Corinth, ally of Sparta. Pericles witnessed only the earlier episodes of the war. To begin with he had some success; but after several reverses the Athenians imposed a fine on him and withdrew his authority (430); only to restore it at the end of the same year. He died not long after from the plague which was ravaging Athens. Pericles was a lover of letters, arts and crafts, and in his century they made their greatest strides: hence the epoch is often known as the "century of Pericles". To the end of his days he led a simple and retired life in the company of philosophers: Anaxagoras, Protagoras, Zeno of Elia, Socrates, Damon the musician, Pheidias the sculptor, Aspasia the hetaira.

Periegetics

Ancient travellers (similar to our modern tourists) who visited different countries and often wrote down their impressions. Pausanias was one of the most famous.

Phoenicians

People of Canaanite origin who came from the shores of the Persian gulf and settled on the Mediterranean littoral at the foot of Lebanon, in about the twenty-fourth century B.C. They founded maritime cities from which their fleets set out to trade and establish colonies throughout the Mediterranean basin, the Red Sea and the Atlantic. They introduced the Mediterranean people to commerce, industry, and navigation, and disseminated an alphabet from which most of the alphabets of the ancient world derive.

Pheidias

The greatest sculptor of Antiquity, born in Attica about 490. He seems first to have addressed himself to painting and then worked, together with Miron and Polykleitas, under the direction of Hegias. He was commissioned to sculpt a statue of Athena for the temple of Plataea, a monument in honour of Militiades at Delphi, the statues of Athena Lemnia and Athena Promachos on the Acropolis. He was appointed superintendent of all the artistic work undertaken by order of the people and, in concert with Pericles, enriched Athens with many beautiful buildings, the Parthenon among them. The metopes, friezes and pediments of this temple were sculpted by him or his staff of collaborators. His two best known statues were the colossal "Zeus" at Olympia (10 m. high), executed in gold and ivory and the "Athena Parthenos", which was destined for the interior of the Parthenon and made of the same materials. Pheidias was accused by Pericles' enemies of having embezzled some of the gold set aside for the statue of Athena; he had to flee Athens and died at Elis, after some years in exile. His works were characterised by nobility, serenity and sublimity. He has been described as the Homer of sculpture.

Philip II

King of Macedon, born about 382 B.C. After coming to the throne he started to seize Greek cities on the Macedonian coast. Despite warnings from Demosthenes, the Athenians refused to be disturbed by this expansionist policy. They were defeated at Chaeronea in 338 B.C., a date which marks the end of Greek independence. Philip was preparing to march against the Persians when

185

he was assassinated by a young noble-man named Pausanias, during the cele-bration of his nuptials with Cleopatra the Macedonian; he had repudiated his first wife, Olympias, the mother of the son who became Alexander the Great.

Philoxenos of Eretria

(Third century B.C.) Disciple of Niko-machos; according to Pliny he painted amongst other things a Bacchic scene with three Silenus figures and a *Battle of Darius with Alexander*, for king Cassander. The famous mosaic in the house of the Faun at Pompeii seems to have been inspired by this latter.

Phintias

Painter potter living in the late sixth-early fifth century B.C. Contemporary of Prygos, Euthimides and Douris.

Phocaea

Ancient Greek city in Asia Minor. One of the twelve great cities of Ionia. Very prosperous, it founded settlements at Elea (Italy), Aleria (Corsica) and Massilia (Gaul), afterwards Marseilles.

Phocis

Territory of ancient Greece between Thessaly and Boeotia. The temple of Delphi, the Oracle of Apollo and Mount Parnassos made Phocis holy ground,

hence the numerous religious wars with which it was troubled, symptomatic of the rivalries between cities who were anxious to lay hands on the territory and the sacred oracle in particular.

Phylakopi

Ancient town on the island of Melos, the first to prosper on the island, from the middle of the third millennium B.C. The British School at Athens has brought to light the remains of three prehistoric cities, the third of which (1500-1100), dating from the Mycenaean period, represents the apogee of the Cycladic civilisation of Melos. Excavations in this archaeological stratum have disclosed traces of a palace with many fresco fragments. Phylakopi was destroyed by the Dorians in 1100 B.C.

Pindus

Chain of mountains in the north of Greece, between Thessaly and Epirus. One of its outcrops forms the Parnassus range and leads to the Helicon range. Pindus was sacred to Apollo and the Muses.

Pistoxenos

Potter working at the end of the fifth century B.C.

Pitsa

Place close to Corinth where the only known paintings on wood were discovered, in a cave (last quarter of the sixth century B.C.).

Plataea

Ancient city of Boeotia, where Pausanias and Aristides defeated the troops of Mardonios, Xerxes' general, in 479 B.C. The Eleutherian or freedom festivals were instituted in memory of this battle, to honour those who died for Greece; they were held every four years. Destroyed by the Thebans in 373 B.C., the city was rebuilt on the orders of Philip II, after the battle of Chaeronea in 338 B.C.

Plato

(427?-348 B.C.) Famous Greek philosopher, born at Aegina. Said to be descended on his father's side from Kodros, on his mother's from Solon. Having become acquainted with Socrates at the age of twenty, he devoted his whole life to philosophy. After the death of his master he spent much time in travel and visited Egypt, Cyrenaica, Magna Graeca and Sicily. Sold as a slave by Dionysios, tyrant of Syracuse who had been outraged by his criticisms, he was bought back into freedom by a certain Anniceris. On his return he decided to settle at Athens. There he founded, in a gymnasium adjoining the groves of Academos, a philosophical school, the Academy. Plato did not want

for an audience. Mentioned among those who became his disciples or attended his lectures are: Xenocrates, Aristotle, Xenophon, Antisthenes, Aristippos, Diogenes, Phaedo, Aeschines, Lykourgos, Demosthenes, etc. Plato's achievement is contained in thirty-six works, nearly all of them dialogues. The characters of the participants are delineated as though in a play. His work divides into two groups: in the first he develops the teaching of Socrates, in the second he expounds his own theories. According to Plato, in addition to God and matter there exist certain universal types from which all beings have taken their forms; these he called "ideas". In the world, only the "ideas" have a real and absolute existence, individual things are but shadows or copies of the ideas. The human soul knows the world of ideas before birth but forgets it on entering the body. The senses take in only the particular, the individual; "ideas", however, can be perceived afresh by a superior faculty, that is to say reason or understanding. The "ideas" reside in God, who is their common substance.

Pliny the Elder

One of the most famous naturalists of Antiquity. Born in 25 A.D. at Como. He served in Germany, made a reputation at the Roman bar, in 68 became procurator of Hispania Citerior and in 75 prefect of the fleet at Misenum. Eager to observe the eruption of Vesuvius, he approached too close and died from suffocation by the burning vapours. Of all his numerous writings, only his "Natural History", in thirty-seven books, has survived. It is a kind of encyclopedia, covering all the learning of his age. The great virtue of Pliny is that he retails to us ideas borrowed from more than two thousand authors. Book XXXV, devoted to painting and colours, contains precious information concerning the paintings of Antiquity.

Plutarch

Born at Chaeronea between 45 and 50 A.D. Greek historian and moralist. He studied at Athens and travelled in Asia and Egypt; he had two sojourns at Rome, where he taught philosophy in public and seems to have been the tutor of Hadrian. In his old age he retired to Chaeronea, where he acted as priest of Apollo during the Delphic festivals. He was the author of numerous writings, collected in the "Ethical works" and "Parallel Lives". His learning is immense and his narrative talent quite exceptional.

Polykleitas

Sculptor of the second half of the fifth

century B.C., born at Sikyon or Argos. He inherited all the traditions of the Argive school and executed most of his masterpieces, nearly all of them representations of athletes, in bronze. He instituted a system of fixed proportions between the different parts of the human body. Statues such as his "Diadoumenos" and still more his "Doryphoros" show the application of this mathematical system. The Polykleitan athlete was to be the model inspiring the majority of sculptors who succeeded him, down to the end of Antiquity. Polykleitas also expounded his plastic ideas in a theoretical treatise on the "Canon" (the rule). He was the friend of Aeschylus, and all contemporary Greek thinkers pay him tribute.

Polygnotos

One of the greatest of all Greek artists. Fresco painter, native of the island of

Thasos. Until the middle of the fifth century B.C. he worked at Athens, where he had founded a school, and it is said that Mikon, Panainos, brother of Pheidias, and Pheidias himself were among his pupils. He was the son of the painter Aglaophon, credited with the first presentation of a *Wingless Victory*. He had links with the family of Kimon, whose sister Elpinike became his mistress. He executed a number of works for several Greek cities. At Athens, he decorated the temple of Theseus (scene from the nuptials of the daughters of Leucippos) and the Poikile, in collaboration with Panainos and Mikon (*The Achaeans on the day after his capture of Troy* and the *Judgment of Ajax*). But his most famous work, described in detail by Pausanias, was in the lesche of the Cnidians at Delphi. These were two frescoes representing the *Sack of Troy* and *Ulysses' visit to Hades*. Some of his works for Athens were executed without payment and earned him from the deme the title of Athenian citizen (he was in fact a metic). Plato showed him great esteem and Aristotle considered him the embodiment of his artistic theory. Polygnotos created the large-scale historical painting. His works often inspired vase painters (cf. the krater of Orvieto in the Louvre, which shows the massacre of the Niobids).

Pontus Euxinus, The Black Sea

Pontus Euxinus, friendly sea: name given to the Black Sea by the Ancients as a euphemism, to avert the dangers of this mist-ridden and often stormy stretch of water by a name of good omen.

Posidonios

(135-50 B.C.) Stoic historian and philosopher, born at Apamea in Syria. He travelled in Spain, Italy, Sicily, Dalmatia, Illyria, Gallia Narbonensis and Liguria, settling about 102 in Rhodes where he was accepted as a citizen, opened a school and taught with such brilliance that very distinguished foreigners came to hear him, Pompey and Cicero among their number. Versed in mathematics, physics and astronomy as well as in philosophy, Posidonios tried to measure the diameter of the earth and of the sun, constructed a celestial sphere, noticed the connection between the tides and the positions of the moon and suspected that they were affected by the moon's movement. As a philosopher he was an eclectic Stoic. He tried to reconcile the teachings of Zeno with the principles of Plato and Aristotle. He was the author of several works, amongst others treatises on "The Soul", "The Gods", "Duty", "Physics", "The Sea", which have not come down to us. He wrote some historical essays which are also lost. Cicero's "On the Nature of the Gods" and "On Fate" are in imitation of Posidonios.

Praxiteles

(c. 390 B.C.-330). Born at Athens, he was probably the son of the sculptor Kephisodotos. It is thought that he travelled in the Peloponnese and in Asia. He had a liaison with the courtesan Phryne. Praxiteles is the supreme master of grace, of feminine and adolescent beauty. He is magnificent in expressing

porches giving access to sacred enclosures
or important buildings. The Propylaea of
the acropolis at Athens formed part of
the citadel and were its principal entrance.
They were built in the time of Pericles
to drawings made by Mnesikles. The
construction consisted of a decorated
facade with six columns of the Ionic order
and magnificent frontispieces.

Protagoras

Born about 500 B.C. at Abdera in Thrace.
In his youth had been a porter. Became
the disciple of Demokritos, taught
rhetoric, grammar and poetry, first at
Abdera and later at Athens. He was the
first to make his lessons pay and became
very rich. He travelled through the cities
of Greece, Sicily and Magna Graeca,
made laws for Thurii and then returned
to live in Athens. Accused by the
Athenians of impiety, he took flight by
boat and was drowned. Protagoras is
representative of the leading sophists,
philosophers who denied the existence
of absolute truths. He said "man is the
measure of all things". He is at the source
of scepticism, relativism and subjective
idealism. The principal lesson he taught
was the art of persuasion. Plato turned
his spot-light on this sophist and refuted
his errors.

the softness of a countenance, tender
emotions. He tends to humanise divine
types. He brought the technique of
working marble to its perfection. His
statues were often touched up with
colour by the painter Nikias. His master-
pieces include: the "Eros of Thespiai",
the "Satyr in repose", the "Apollo
Sauroktonos", the "Hermes carrying the
infant Dionysos" and various "Aphro-
dites", for which Phryne served as a
model ("Aphrodite of Thespiai", "of
Cos", "of Cnidos", etc.). Apart from
two originals, these works are known
only from copies. Praxiteles had numerous pupils. He had a considerable
influence, not only on the development
of sculpture but also on Attic stelae and
Tanagra figurines.

Protogenos

Greek painter of the second half of the
fourth century B.C., native of Caunos in
Caria. Lived chiefly on the island of
Rhodes. He was considered the rival of

Propylaea

Greek word signifying the vestibules or

Apelles. When Demetrius Poliorcetes was besieging Rhodes about the year 304, he gave orders that the quarter containing his studio was to be spared. It is said that Protogenos took eleven years to paint his picture of *Ialysos*, depicting the hero-guardian of the Rhodian city of the same name. This picture was later removed to Rome, to the temple of Peace. Among other paintings mention is made of portraits of Alexander the Great, of the mother of Aristotle, of king Antigonos, and some mythological subjects: *Satyr in repose*, *Pan*, *Cydippe* and *Tlepolemus*. The Propylaea of Athens carried a picture of him representing "Paralos" and "Ammonias", the two sacred galleys or the heroes of the same name; and in the chamber of the Council of the Five Hundred there was a picture of the *College of the Thesmothetai*. Protogenos also executed statues in bronze.

Prytaneion

Building at Athens in which the fifty members of the Boule invested for the time being with the title of prytanis met and were maintained at the public expense. Permanently in session at this spot, the prytanes could watch over the safety of the state, warn the other Boule members of any dangers and summon them at need. The prytaneion was also the place where public meals, available to those who had earned the right to be fed at the expense of the state, were distributed. When the judges asked Socrates what punishment he deserved he replied, "To be fed in the prytaneion for the rest of my days". The prytanaea also served as the public granary; the penates of the state were lodged and venerated there and the Vestal fire kept alight.

Pylos

Ancient town of the Peloponnesos. It was the capital of one of the great states of the heroic epoch, that of the Nelides, contemporaries of the Atrides of Mycenae, the most famous of whom was Nestor the wise, who took part in the Trojan war. Recent excavations have made it possible to uncover what may well have been his palace and have yielded a number of inscribed tablets.

191

Rhodes

(From Greek "rodon", rose, because of the host of rose bushes growing wild there.) Island in the Aegean, off the south-west coast of Anatolia, the principal of the group called the Dodecanese. In prehistoric times it was settled by emigrants from Crete and the mainland, as is proved by the necropoleis of Ialysos and Camiros, where pottery discovered attests a Creto-Mycenaean

influence. About 1100 B.C. the Dorians became established there and founded the three cities of Ialysos, Lindos and Rhodes. Rhodes was famed in Antiquity for the purity of its air and the excellence of its fruit. Subject first to Athens and later to Sparta, it afterwards became independent, a powerful republic whose fleet dominated the seas. Rhodes despatched colonists to Sicily, Italy and Spain. The grandeur and beauty of its works of art made it famous throughout Greece. The famous Colossus (Apollo or the Sun), an enormous brass statue 70 cubits high, was considered one of the seven wonders of the world. The maritime laws of Rhodes were in force along all the coasts and in all the ports of the Mediterranean; they became the foundation of all national maritime codes.

Rhodopi

Small village near Chania (Crete). In 1942 German archeologists brought to light there ruins of a sanctuary of the second century A.D. consecrated to Artemis Diktynna, Hellenistic period.

Rhoikos

Greek architect and sculptor from Samos. Father of Theodoros and alleged to have collaborated with him in directing the building of the great temple of Hera at Samos and of the first temple of Artemis at Ephesus, both assigned to about the year 600 B.C. As sculptors, Rhoikos and his son are supposed to have introduced from Egypt the art of applying bronze casting to statuary.

Samos

Greek island in the Aegean archipelago near the coast of Asia Minor. In the archaic period the Samians were famed as metallurgists and goldsmiths (Rhoikos and Theodoros of Samos were the first to practice hollow-casting in bronze) and also as engineers and architects. Liberated from the Persians by the Treaty of 479 B.C., Samos joined the Athenian alliance, revolting against it without success in 440. Under the Treaty of Antalkidas (387) Samos again fell into Persian hands. During the Hellenistic period she was subject to garrisons from Egypt, Syria and Pergamun.

Sarcophagus

(From Greek "sarx", flesh and "phago", I devour.) Boxes made of stone or wood in which the ancients deposited corpses they did not wish to burn. The etymology of the word is explained by the fact that it originally designated boxes made from a specific stone from Assos, which according to Pliny had the property of consuming the body within the space of forty days.

Saurias of Samos

(Seventh century B.C.) Considered one of the inventors of linear painting. A tale was current about him similar to that told of the legendary young woman of Corinth, who traced round the shadow cast on a wall by the profile of her lover and thus provided the contour for the first bas-relief.

Sikyon

Or 'city of gourds' (modern Kiato), very close to Patras. Ancient site founded in the second millennium B.C. by the Ionians, later conquered by the Dorians. Governed first by the Orthagorid dynasty, Sikyon was later a prey to factions and fell under tyrants; from the Peloponnesian war the ally of Sparta, was captured by Epaminondas and became subject to Macedon. Sikyon was destroyed and then rebuilt by Demetrius Poliorcetes (303). It then formed part of the Achaean League. The city is famous for its schools of sculptors, bronze-smiths, painters and potters.

Simonides of Chios or Cos

(About 556-467 B.C.) Greek lyric poet. The ancients made much of his work and ranked him with Pindar. He composed epigrams, odes, elegies, plays, threnodies (poems chanted at the obsequies of great personages) and several epic poems. Only fragments of his work survive.

193

Skopas

Greek sulptor and architect of the fourth century B.C. Born at Paros, emigrated while still very young to the Peloponneses and in the course of his life worked in several cities of the Greek world. He executed an "Aphrodite Pandermos" at Elis, a "Hecate" at Argos and an "Asklepios" and a "Hygieia" at Gortys in Arcadia. The Tegeans then entrusted him with the building and decoration of the temple of Athena Alea, whose pediments, showing "The Hunt for the Calydon Boar" and the "Fight between Achilles and Telephus" were especially admired. He also collaborated in the famous mausoleum of Halicarnassus and the temple of Artemis at Ephesus. He sculpted two "Erinnyes" for the temple of the Furies close to the acropolis at Athens. The ancient authors cite numerous other works: a "Bacchante tearing a kid", known from a marble replica preserved at Dresden, a "Lyre-playing Apollo" at Rhammonte, "Eros, Pothos and Himeros" at Megara, a "Dionysos" in marble at Knidos, an "Aphrodite and Pothos" at Samothrace, a "Sminthian Apollo" at Chrysa in the Troad, etc. Animation, pathos, energy in execution appear to have been his outstanding qualities and the ancients show no hesitation in comparing him with Praxiteles and even with Pheidias.

Slip

Earthy coating, white or coloured, which potters use to cover a ceramic paste, to mask its natural colouring. This procedure was known to the ancient Greeks. They knew how to scratch the slip in places to make incised designs by uncovering the underlying paste.

Smyrna

City of Asia Minor. Flourishing port on the Aegean. Founded by the Aeolians before the seventh century B.C. Smyrna repulsed the attacks of Gyges, king of Lydia, but was destroyed by Alyattes. Rebuilt by Alexander, it took on a splendid new lease of life.

Socrates

Greek philosopher born at Athens about 470 B.C., died 399. Son of the sculptor Sophroniscos and Phainarete, a midwife. At first worked with his father, then became the pupil of Prodicos and of the geometer Theodore of Cyrene. He also studied the maxims of the old sageas and adopted the celebrated precept "Know thyself"; from this time on he is shown going to and fro in Athens, in the market place, in the gymnasia, in the tradesmen's workshops, conversing with those he met about the principles of their art or craft, the basis of the laws, domestic economy, duties, the God who showed such order and wisdom in his disposition of the world; declaring war on prejudice and vice, stimulating minds and improving manners. To confound the sophists, he posed them questions they found embarrassing, a kind of close-knit interrogation which has been called "Socratic irony". Another of his methods,

"maieutics" (or intellectual midwifery) consisted in eliciting from the people he engaged in conversation knowledge of which they were ignorant but which was really latent in the bottom of their minds. Socrates rescued Alcibiades when he was wounded in the siege of Potidaea. He showed his courage at Delium (424) and at Amphibolis (423). At a fairly advanced age he became a member of the Senate and carried out his new functions with his accustomed justness and resolution. He knew how to stand up to the Thirty Tyrants who had usurped power in the state and never ceased to reproach them for their iniquities and crimes. But the freedom of his discource and the sublimity of his genius made him numerous enemies. In 400 Meletos, Lycon and Anytos accused him of impiety and corrupting the youth. The philosopher was condemned to death by the Council of the Five Hundred. His respect for the laws of his country was such that he refused to escape. Surrounded by his dismayed disciples, he swallowed with serenity the hemlock proffered to him by the State executioner. Although Socrates wrote nothing, although he had no school properly speaking, he was nevertheless the real founder of moral science. He replaced the sophistical methods of his philosophical predecessors by true self-knowledge. He upheld the existence of an absolute truth which can be attained by abandoning every particular interest and reaching out towards general concepts. Plato, Xenophon, Aristippos and Antisthenes were his most brilliant disciples.

Solon

(About 640-558 B.C.) Athenian statesman, born at Salamis. Descended from Codrus. Visited Greece, Egypt and Asia. He was numbered among the seven sages and his fame was further enhanced by his poetry. He was charged with the reform of the laws of his country and appointed sole archon in 594. He divided the citizens into four classes, according to their wealth; all together made up the Popular Assembly, which possessed the greatest powers. But the magistrates could be elected only from the first three classes. The judges or heliasts were chosen each year by lot from all the classes. Solon established or brought order into the Senate and the Areopagus. He retained the archon system. The tables of Solon were a comprehensive legislative code, considerable fragments of which survive. Foreigners—metics—were attracted to Athens and it was easy for them to become citizens. Slaves were more humanly treated. After being

195

absent on his travels for ten years, Solon returned to find Athens disturbed by factions and made vain efforts at preventing Peisistratos from seizing power. He lived on, respected by Peisistratos, who upheld his laws, and occupying himself solely with his poetry. His legislation, very fruitful in consequences, was in part responsible for the brilliant destiny of Athens.

Sophilos

(First quarter of the sixth century B.C.) Painter potter, contemporary with Timonidas of Corinth. One of the earliest whose name is known with any certainty. His name appears on a few vases ("Dinos from the Acropolis of Athens", "Dinos of Pharsalos", etc.).

Sophocles

(Athens, 497-406 B.C.) One of the three great tragic poets of Greece. Born of a relatively powerful family. His father, Sophilos, was head of a weapon factory. Very wealthy, he gave his son a substantial education. About 480 Sophocles was chosen on account of his beauty to conduct the choir of young men in the "Paean" chanted after the victory of Salamis. At the age of twenty-seven he competed for the tragedy prize and defeated Aeschylus. It is said that he won it twenty times. In 440 Sophocles was elected as the general to command the expedition to Samos. Later he exercised other public functions. The ancients credit him with the authorship of 123

plays. Only seven survive, but they are probably his finest: "Antigone", "Electra", "The Trachinian Women", "Oedipus Rex", "Ajax", "Philoctetus" and "Oedipus at Colonus". Sophocles is interested above all in the portrayal of character: he is the founder of psychological drama. He brought greater flexibility and variety into the language of drama. His style is elegant, rich, poetic in the lyrical portions, precise and vigorous in the dialogue. He was the Athenian poet *par excellence*.

Sotades

(Second quarter of the fifth century B.C.) Potter. Probably the author of three footed cups, one of which is signed. He is thought to be identical with the artist known by convention as the "Sotades painter".

Sparta or Lacedaemon

Famous city of ancient Greece on the river Eurotas. Capital of Laconia and the Republic of Sparta. The legislator Lykourgos (late ninth century B.C.) laid the foundations of an oligarchical and militarist state which remained fixed over the centuries, becoming anachronistic towards the end of its existence. This strongly aristocratic and military constitution made Sparta into a war machine in a state of continual readiness and trained on its neighbours. Sparta was the enemy of the democracies, above all Athens. The two Messenian wars (743-723, 685-668) gave Sparta possession of all the southern Peloponnesos. Tegea was made subject and the Argolis conquered, with the exception of Argos; Corinth and the Elis recognised Spartan supremacy and Athens was attacked in 510. Sparta played an important part in the Persian wars, until the moment when Athens took first place. The rivalry between the two republics came to a head in the Peloponnesian war (431-404). Victorious thanks to Persian aid, Sparta subjected the Greeks to an imperious and arbitrary rule; showing little gratitude for past help, Sparta even attacked those who had assisted her to triumph. This policy resulted in the expeditions led by Clearchos, Thymbron, Dercyllias and Agesilas (401-395). But the agents of the Persian king were dispensing gold throughout Greece, where malcontents were numerous, and brought into being a league formed by Athens, Argos, Corinth and Thebes. Sparta, feeling her power menaced, signed with the great king the shameful treaty of Antalkidas (387), which she hoped would allow her to tyrannise Greece at leisure. But Thebes, led by Pelopidas and Epaminondas, inflicted blows on Sparta from which she would never recover. When Sparta was desirous of attacking Messene and Megalopolis, Philip, king of Macedon, forced her to retreat within her own bounds (350). She left Philip to overwhelm the Greeks at Chaeronea, refused to acknowledge his title of generalissimo against the Persians, took no part in Alexander's expedition and even attacked Macedon in his absence. But king Agis III was defeated and killed by Antipater. From that time onward Sparta played only a secondary role.

Stoa

Covered colonnaded portico, often decorated with frescoes, serving as a place for strolling and meeting people.

Strabo

(65? B.C.-20 A.D.) Greek geographer born at Amiseia in Asia Minor. He early on conceived the idea of a large-scale geographical work, travelled the greater part of the then known world and on returning to Amiseia composed two treatises:'Historical memorials" in forty-four books, no longer extant, and a

Wall painting
"Tomb of the Funeral Couch" (detail)
460 B.C.
Young men holding back a race-horse
Tarquinia, necropolis

"Geography which we have almost in its entirety. Strabo does not content himself with a bare reference to names and locations. He gives numerous judicious details concerning the history, customs and institutions of the people, their origins and their traditions.

Tarentum

City of southern Italy on the gulf of the same name. It was founded about 708 B.C. by Parthenians expelled from Sparta and became one of the most important cities of Magna Graeca.

Susiane

Ancient province of the Persian empire, bordered on the north by Media, on the south by the Persian gulf. Its capital was Susa. Susiane was the centre of the kingdom of Elam, formed a satrapy of the Persian Empire and after the death of Alexander became part of the Kingdom of Syria. It was captured from the Syrian kings by the Parthians.

Tarquinia

The most ancient city of Etruria (ninth century B.C.), in the valley of the Marta. In the eight and seventh centuries it was the Etruscan political and religious centre. Important funerary remains have been discovered there, in particular decorated tombs (Tombs of Hunting and Fishing, the Triclinium, the Typhon, the Funeral Couch, the Baron, the Shields, Orcus of Francesca Questimani, etc.).

Taygetus

Range of mountains in the Peloponnesos, close to Sparta. The Spartans threw infants born defective from the top of its chief peak.

Syracuse

Town in Sicily, with a port, on the east coast of the island. Fatherland of Archimedes and Theocritos. Founded by the Corinthians, it was one of the oldest and largest Greek colonies in Sicily. A turbulent republic, governed by kings or tyrants—Gelon, Hieron, the two Dionysios, Hiero II—it was taken by the Romans in 212.

Telephanes of Sikyon

(Seventh century B.C.) See "Kleanthes of Corinth".

Thalassocracy

(From Greek "thalassa", sea, and "kratos", empire.) Absolute command of the seas.

Thebes

Ancient capital of Boeotia founded according to tradition by Cadmos the Phoenician. From heroic times, Thebes was the scene of innumerable dramatic legends, which inspired Aeschylus, Sophocles, Euripides. Victorious over Sparta thanks to Pelopidas and Epaminondas, Thebes enjoyed a brief period of glory during which she imposed her hegemony on the city-states of Greece. But her power soon evaporated. Thebans and Athenians came together at the urging of Demosthenes, to be defeated by Philip of Macedon at Chaeronea in 338. Alexander destroyed their city, sparing only the house of Pindar (335). Cassander rebuilt it, but the citizens henceforth were famous only for their lengthy banquets and thick wits.

Theophrastos

Born at Lesbos (372?-287 B.C.). Greek scholar and philosopher. His name was actually Tyrtamos, but he was called Theophrastos ("divine orator") because of his dazzling eloquence. A disciple of Aristotle, he succeeded him in the direction of the Lyceum. Two large works of his have survived: "The History of Plants" and the "Characters". This latter was imitated by La Bruyére.

Thera

(Santorin.) Island in the Cyclades. On several occasions the scene of volcanic activity. Thera was colonised by the Phoenicians about the year 2000, then by the Dorians. Later the Ptolemies made it a naval base for the Aegean Sea.

Thermos

Ancient Greek town in Aetolia, close to Agrinion. Nothing has survived of the town which contained the rich sanctuary of Apollo, centre of the Aetolian League. It was sacked and destroyed in 207 B.C. by Philip V of Macedon, who carried off two thousand statues in his booty. The temple of Apollo Thermios had some unusual painted metopes (sixth century) as part of its decoration.

Thespiai

Ancient Boeotian town, close to Thebes, at the foot of the Helicon range. Its remains were explored between 1888 and 1891 by the Ecole française. Nothing survives of the ancient enclosure, but the foundations of the temple of the Muses mentioned by Pausanias have been discovered.

Thessaly

Territory of ancient Greece between the Pindos, Phocis and the sea; principal towns Larissa, Pharsalos, Pherae and Lamia. Populated initially by the Pelasgi, it was later invaded by the Achaeans and the Dorians. In the fifth century Thessaly was disturbed by quarrels between rival families (the Alenades of Pherae, the Echechraticles of Pharsalos, the Scopades of Krannon). At the time of the Persian wars, the Alenades submitted to Xerxes and led his army. After the peace of Antalkidas, Jason, tyrant of Pherae, aimed to subdue Sparta and have himself proclaimed leader of the Greeks against the Persians; he was assassinated. Philip of Macedon divided and subjected Thessaly in 357.

Thucydides

Athenian historian, born in the deme of Halimos (Attica) about 456 B.C., died after 395. Son of Oloros, related both to the family of Miltiades and to that of Oloros, king of Thrace. Appointed strategos, he served in the Peloponnesian war and was entrusted with the relief of Amphipolis and Eion; saving only the former of these towns, he was punished with banishment. His exile lasted twenty years. He passed them in Thrace at Skapte Hyle, where he had some gold mines, and employed them to collect materials for his "History of the Peloponnesian War". To the ancients he was The Historian *par excellence;* the moderns have confirmed their judgment. He is admired for his critical method, with its high degree of impartiality. He is considered the founder of scientific history. His style is remarkable for its vigour and extreme conciseness of expression.

Tiberius

(42 B.C.-37 A.D.) Roman emperor, son of Tiberius Claudius Nero and Livia Drusilla, who was also descended from the "gens Claudia". When Octavian married Livia, Tiberius and his brother Drusus were raised to the imperial family. Augustus married Tiberius to Vipsania Agrippina, daughter of Agrippa. Tiberius and Drusus were sent to complete the conquest of Rhaetia and Vindelicia (15 B.C.) and in 13 B.C. Tiberius held the consulship. After the death of Agrippa, Augustus forced him to repudiate his wife and marry Julia, Agrippa's widow (12 B.C.). Tiberius conducted three fine campaigns in Pannonia, commanded the Rhine army and obtained the title imperator, together with the consulship, in 7 B.C., and afterwards five years of tribunician power (6 B.C.). But he was jealous of the affection Augustus showed for his grandsons and retired to Rhodes. He was given leave to return to Rome (A.D. 2) and was adopted by the emperor (A.D. 4). He commanded the Rhine army and pacified the region between the Danube and the Adriatic. The death of Augustus (A.D. 14) brought him the empire. He exerted his authority in a decisive manner. He made Sejanus, Praetorian Prefect, his chief minister, and then retired to Campania (21). Crimes and executions

multiplied. Tiberius next settled on the island of Capri, where the Romans, perhaps without justification, accused him of indulging in infamous debaucheries. Sejanus, meanwhile, had aroused Tiberius' suspicions. The emperor had him arrested in full Senate and put to death by Macro, 31. He then inflicted atrocities on the friends and allies of the minister, all the more when he learned that his son had been poisoned, but he was no more merciful to the family of Germanicus. The provinces continued to be governed with the greatest moderation. In 37 he fell ill in Campania and was forced to halt at Misenum, in the villa of Lucullus. Macro thought he was dead and was proclaiming Caligula his successor, but the emperor revived; whereupon the Praetorian Prefect had him suffocated by his bed coverings.

Tiber

Anciently Tiberinus, river of central Italy which passes through Rome and debouches into the Tyrrhenian sea. The Romans from a very early date deified the river which watered their city. They imagined that before becoming god of the river Tiberinus had been king of the country. He thus played a role in the legendary foundation of Rome. The story went that he had married the Vestal Rhea Silvia, mother of Romulus and Remus, after she had thrown herself into the waters of the river on the orders of her uncle Amulius.

Timonidas of Corinth

(First quarter of the six century B.C.) Painter potter, contemporary with Sophilos.

Tiryns

With Mycenne, one of the most ancient and most celebrated towns of the Argolis. Enclosed by fortifications from the third millennium B.C., it reached its zenith in the second millennium. Presumed fatherland of Herakles. Famous for its Cyclopean walls whose construction is still admired today.

Titus Livius (Livy)

(59 B.C.-17 A.D.) Latin historian, born at Padua. He was brought to Rome by Augustus who admitted him to his intimate circle. He composed a "History of Rome" in 144 books, only 25 of which have come down to us. His work is very important for its information concerning the first centuries of the Republic.

Troy

Ilion or Pergama, city of Asia Minor. Capital of the Troad, near the shore of the Hellespont. The Trojan war, immortalised by Homer, is the most celebrated event of mythological times. It was occasioned by the outrage Paris, son of the Trojan king Priam, inflicted on Menelaus in abducting his wife Helen.

Tylissos

Place near Heraklion (Crete) at the foot of Mount Ida.

The "Chigi" oenochoe (detail)
Provenance Formella, close to Veii (Etruria)
Third quarter of 7th century
Lion Hunt
Rome, Villa Giulia

Vassiliki

Place in the eastern part of Crete. Amongst other discoveries, an important mansion with twenty-two rooms dating from Old Minoan II. The vases known as Vassiliki are of the special "flamed" type.

Veii

One of the most powerful cities of the Etruscan Confederation. Famous for its dramatic conflicts with Rome in which it was completely demolished after a ten years' siege (396 B.C.). Veii possessed a sanctuary dedicated to the cult of waters, which has yielded terracotta statues derived from the school of Vulca. Veii was in fact the most important Etruscan centre for the manufacture of clay figurines. The most ancient paintings of

the classical world were also discovered here (Campana Tomb).

Vitruvius

Roman architect born at Verona or Formiae about 85 B.C. Julius Caesar employed him to build engines of war. Author of a classic treatise "On Architecture". This book is precious, since it not only deals with architecture and describes monuments existing in his day, but also touches on all the subjects with a bearing on architecture: mechanics, hydraulics and gnomonics.

Volsinii

An important Etrurian lucumony, known chiefly thanks to the Greek and Latin historians. Its territory contained the federal sanctuary, the Fanum Voltumnae, where the festivals uniting all the members of the confederation were celebrated each year. The site of this town has not been identified with any certainty. It was probably on a hill dominating Bolsena, where a large necropolis and the remains of walls have been discovered.

Vulci

Etruscan city in the region of the Maremma. It attained its apogee in the sixth century B.C. and must have been fabulously wealthy, as attested by the thousands of Greek vases found in its necropolis. Its craftsmen excelled in sculpture in stone, bronze work and metallurgy. The famous François Tomb is to be seen in this necropolis.

Bas-relief from the palace at **Persepolis**
Throne of Xerxes, detail
Paris, Louvre

Xerxes

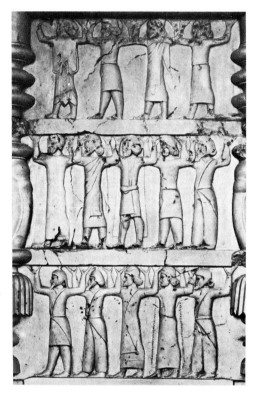

King of Persia from 486-465 B.C., son of
Darius I. Having subjected Egypt, in
480 he resumed the war with Greece. He
received the submission of Macedon and
Thessaly and reached Thermopylae, where
Leonidas made him lose 20,000 men; the
Persian fleet then experienced a further
set-back near the promontory of Arte-
mision and the Greeks, commanded by
Themistocles, destroyed it at Salamis.
Xerxes' land troops, commanded by
Mardonios, were defeated by the Greeks
at Plataea. His fleet was defeated the
same day near the promontory of Mycale,
in 479. Xerxes was assassinated in 465
by a Hyrcanian named Artaban.

Zeuxis

(464?-394 B.C.) One of the most re-
nowned painters of ancient Greece. Born
at Heraklea, he came to Athens as a
young man (about 425) and knew
Socrates. He also spent some time at the
court of king Archelaos of Macedon,
whose palace he decorated. He passed
his closing years at Ephesus. Slow and
painstaking in his art, he dedicated himself to the perfection of the technique of
painting, endeavouring to render the
play of light and shade, sometimes
pressing his concern for exactitude to the
point of *trompe-l'oeuil*. He also executed
paintings in monochrome. He was more
interested in powerful expression and
realism than in psychology. His subjects
were primarily mythological: *The flaying
of Marsyas, The infant Herakles strangling
the serpents* (which was imitated in
several of the Pompeian frescoes), a
*Family of Centaurs, Zeus enthroned, Pan,
Boreas, Triton.* He showed a predilection
for female figures and his *Penelope* and
Helen bathing were much admired. For
this last work, painted at the request of
the inhabitants of Croton, Zeuxis posed
five girls from the town and reproduced
the most perfect feature of each. The still
life of his *Grapes* was so life-like that it is
said even the birds were deceived. His total
achievement had a pround influence on
the vase painters, as also on the decorators
of Herculanum and Pompeii. In the days
of Tiberius fake Zeuxis pictures were
being sold in Rome.

Printed in Switzerland

Bibliography

Greek Painting

J. D. Beazley and B. Ashmole: *Greek Sculpture and Painting*, Cambridge 1932 (second edition 1966).

E. Buschor: *Greek Vase Painting* (translation by G. C. Richards from the first edition, 1921).

J. Charbonneaux: *L'Art égeen*, Paris 1929

S. Karouzou: *The Amasis Painter*, Oxford 1956.

G. Méautis: *Les Chefs-d'Œuvre de la Peinture grecque*, Paris 1939.

G. M. A. Richter: *A Handbook of Greek Art*, London 1959.

M. Robertson: *Greek Painting*, London 1959.

A. Rumpf: *Maleri und Zeichnung*, Munich 1953.

F. Villard: *Les Vases grecs*, Paris 1956.

C. Zervos: *L'Art de la Crète*, Paris 1956.

Etruscan Painting

R. Bloch: *Etruscan Art* (translation by G. Scaglia and J. Templeton), London 1959

P. Ducati: *Storia dell'arte etrusca*, Florence 1927

A. Frova: *L'Art etrusca*, Milan 1957

D. H. Lawrence: *Etruscan Places*, London 1932.

H. Leisinger: *Les peintures étrusques de Tarquinia*, Lausanne 1953.

G. K. Loukomski: *Art étrusque*, Paris 1931

M. Pallottino: *Etruscan Painting* (translated by M. E. Stanley and S. Gilbert), Geneva 1952.

M. Pallottino: *Art of the Etruscans*, 1955.

O.-W. von Vacano: *The Etruscans in the Ancient World* (translated by S. A. Ogilvie), London 1960.

Table of Illustrations

Maps

Dictionary

207

Greek and Etruscan Painting

This third volume in the series History of
Painting was printed by Säuberlin & Pfeiffer,
of Vevey.

The text was
composed in Times 10 point type and the
first and third parts were printed on machine-
coated paper and the second part on blue
cartridge paper.

The cover and lay-out of the inside pages
were designed by Jean-Marie Clerc of
Editions Rencontre.

The volume was bound by Maurice Busenhart
of Lausanne.